A

# SAINSBURY COOKBOOK

—

# THE COOKING OF
## THE
# CARIBBEAN

# ELISABETH
# LAMBERT ORTIZ

# CONTENTS

Published exclusively for J Sainsbury plc
Stamford House Stamford Street
London SE1 9LL
by Martin Books
Simon & Schuster Consumer Group
Grafton House 64 Maids Causeway
Cambridge CB5 8DD

First published 1991
Second impression October 1992

ISBN 0 85941 750 6

Text, photographs and illustrations © 1991,
J Sainsbury plc

# THE AUTHOR

*Alistair Morrison,*
*London*

Elisabeth Lambert Ortiz is the award-winning author of a number of cookbooks covering a wide range of cuisines, including Caribbean, Mexican, Latin American, Japanese, Spanish and Portuguese, French and British.

Her interest in the Caribbean began when she attended school in the West Indies. She made a study of the food of the islands and went on to become principal consultant on the Caribbean for the Time-Life Foods of the World series, also supplying the recipes for the book.

For many years Elisabeth has contributed articles to magazines such as *Gourmet* and *House and Garden* in New York, where she lived when her husband was an official with the United Nations. She spent six years island-hopping during holidays and still regrets the inevitable number of islands missed out of the 200-odd. She visited markets wherever she went and was lucky enough to have friends in many of the island cultures – Dutch, Spanish, French and British.

Elisabeth now lives in London and continues to enjoy cooking Caribbean food.

*Arroz con Pollo (Chicken with rice, page 42)*

*Floating Islands (page 72)*

# INTRODUCTION

The cuisine of the Caribbean is above all eclectic, gathering its ingredients and cooking methods from Europe, Asia and Africa and combining them with its own native foods, which were unknown to the rest of the world until the arrival of Christopher Columbus in 1492. When he discovered the West Indies, Columbus is said to have remarked that there were so many islands he did not know which to visit first. That is hardly any wonder as there are over 200 islands in the 2,600 mile chain that stretches from Florida in the north to Venezuela in the south, and includes the Greater Antilles – Cuba, Jamaica, Hispaniola (shared between Haiti and the Dominican Republic) and Puerto Rico – as well as the smaller islands that make up the Lesser Antilles – the Leeward and Windward islands and the Virgin islands. Columbus was struck by their beauty. The fields, he wrote, were very green and filled with an infinity of fruits, and everywhere there was the perfume of flowers and the sweet sound of birdsong.

In spite of the passing of time and inevitable progress, what Columbus wrote then is still true, as any lover of the Caribbean will agree. I shall always cherish the years I spent in Jamaica as a schoolgirl. My appetite for island food was whetted, never to diminish, and when later I got a chance to make a proper investigation of this multitudinous cuisine I seized on it

*Rum Punch (page 89)*

*Fried Ripe Plantains (page 70)*

*Hot Pepper Relish (page 74)*

joyfully. The beauty of the islands is still as Columbus saw it; the cuisine has been greatly enhanced since his day, with influences from the rest of the world meeting in the cooking pots of thousands of island kitchens. Island food always reminds me of a ballet when the dancers meet and separate and meet again in different combinations, an endless kaleidoscopic pattern. Island food is like that, each encounter a borrowing, the dish enhanced, but never wholly changed.

The original inhabitants of the islands were Amerindians who had emigrated from South America. These were the gentle Arawaks and the fierce Caribs. Some of the Arawaks, expert farming people, brought with them maize and chilli peppers, sweet, pungent and hot, that had first been cultivated in the valley of Mexico, and cassava, yams and sweet potatoes from the South American mainland. They also made an alcoholic drink from maize, *chichita*. This beer-like drink is still made and widely enjoyed in South America as *chicha*. They were good fishermen but did little hunting as there were no large animals in the islands. Mostly they hunted the *agouti* – a small rabbit-like creature, still eaten in Argentina – various birds and sometimes iguanas. For seasonings, apart from peppers and chillies, they had allspice, which is native to the Caribbean. Their culinary influence can still be seen in the islands, where root vegetables like yams and sweet potatoes are immensely popular.

The Caribs, slightly later arrivals, were a warlike lot forever raiding the poor Arawaks who were slowly eliminated. The Caribs lived mostly by hunting birds and fish, when they weren't hunting Arawaks. Some agriculture was carried on, probably by Arawak women captured in Carib raids since only the men were killed. Some Carib dishes are still popular in the islands. They have, of course, been refined over the centuries, but illustrate the persistence of culinary tradition.

The discovery of the West Indies by

## Preparation and cooking times

*Preparation and cooking times are included at the head of the recipes as a general guide; preparation times, especially, are approximate and timings are usually rounded to the nearest 5 minutes.*

*Preparation times include the time taken to prepare ingredients in the list, but not to make any 'basic' recipe, such as coconut milk.*

*The cooking times given at the heads of the recipes denote cooking periods when the dish can be left largely unattended, e.g. baking, stewing, and not the total amount of cooking for the recipe. Always read and follow the timings given for the steps of the recipe in the method.*

## Shopping

*For further information on purchasing dried, bottled and canned ingredients, write to:*
*Enco Products (London) Ltd*
*71–75 Fortess Road*
*London NW5 1AU*

*For further information on purchasing fresh fruit and vegetables, write to:*
*Sunburst Commodity Trading Limited*
*Central Chambers*
*47 High Street*
*Tonbridge*
*Kent TN9 1SD*

Columbus was the prelude to a new era in Caribbean history, when the islands were drawn into the complex rivalries of the European nations as they established their New World empires. During the seventeenth and eighteenth centuries constant warfare among the European colonial powers brought endless changes in governments, with some islands changing hands repeatedly. Jamaica, for example, had first been visited by Columbus in 1494, and again in 1502 when he was forced to beach his ship. In 1509 a colony was set up, largely for cattle-raising which the Spanish introduced into the islands. Spain claimed the islands, but the Dutch, English and French thought differently. The English attacked Jamaica and by 1688 it had become an English island. This was typical of what was going on all over the Caribbean. With every change something of the culinary tradition of the previous ownership seems to have been left behind, hence Jamaica's Caveached Fish (Pickled fish), which is clearly Spanish Escabeche.

Great changes to the islands' culinary as well as economic history came about when African slaves were brought in huge numbers to work the sugar-cane plantations in the sixteenth century. African slaves, Indian and Chinese settlers, and Jewish people expelled from Portugal, have all contributed. It is a paradox that there is a recognisable Caribbean cuisine with so many diverse strains blending, yet remaining separate, with certain basic seasonings and techniques in each national group of islands giving the dishes their characteristic and unmistakable flavours.

The cooking of the French islands has an unmistakable French stamp, so does the cooking of the English islands, both within the Caribbean framework. In Trinidad, strongly influenced by migrant Hindu workers from the Indian sub-continent, dry or wet *massala* (curry powder or paste) and ghee (clarified butter) are much used, and the island has also adopted

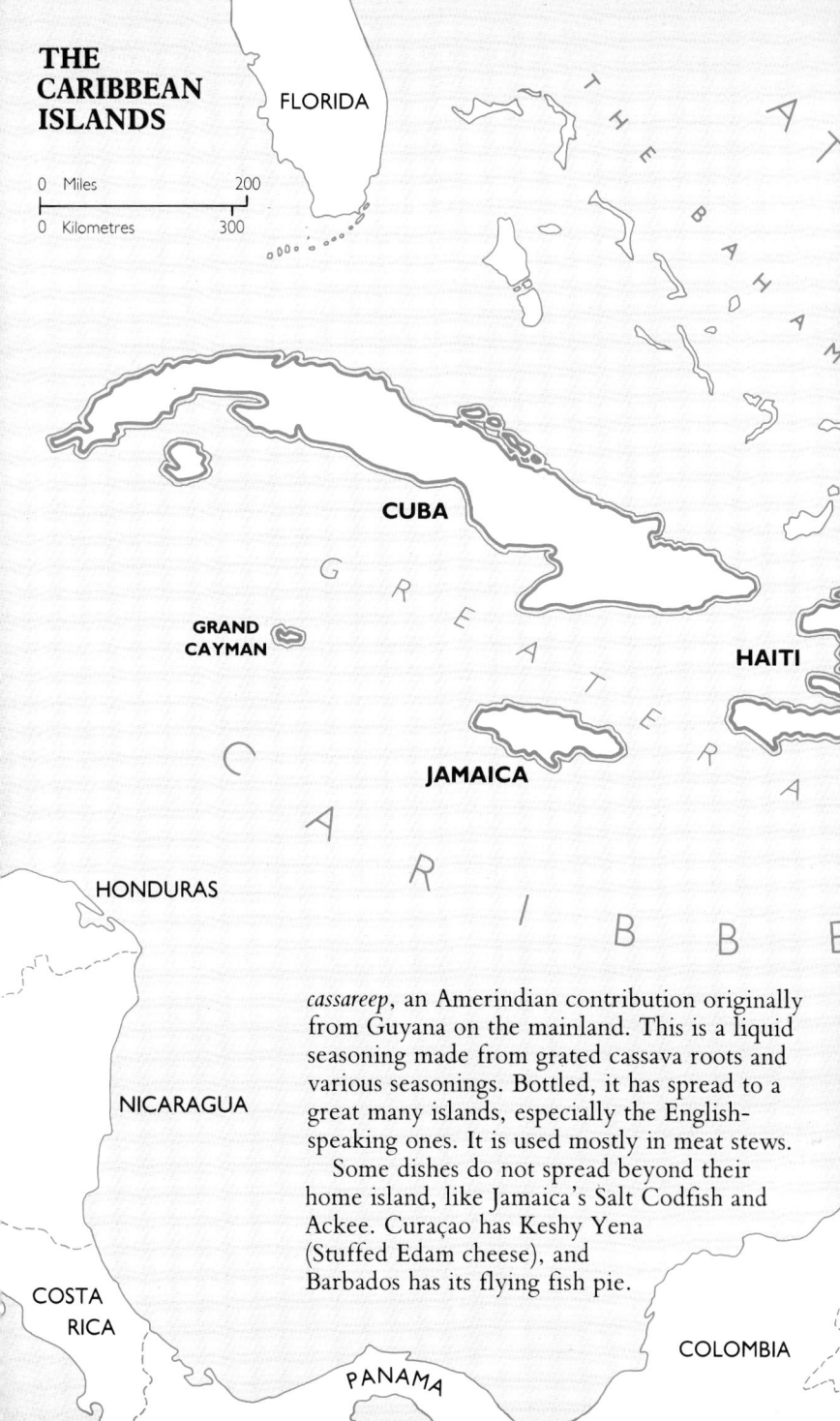

# THE CARIBBEAN ISLANDS

0 Miles 200
0 Kilometres 300

FLORIDA

THE BAHAMA

ATL

CUBA

GRAND CAYMAN

HAITI

GREATER

JAMAICA

CARIBBE

HONDURAS

NICARAGUA

COSTA RICA

PANAMA

COLOMBIA

*cassareep*, an Amerindian contribution originally from Guyana on the mainland. This is a liquid seasoning made from grated cassava roots and various seasonings. Bottled, it has spread to a great many islands, especially the English-speaking ones. It is used mostly in meat stews.

Some dishes do not spread beyond their home island, like Jamaica's Salt Codfish and Ackee. Curaçao has Keshy Yena (Stuffed Edam cheese), and Barbados has its flying fish pie.

The islanders are great travellers so that many dishes do go island-hopping, and are given a warm welcome in their new homes. It is this blending that has created a genuine Caribbean cuisine, a diverse unity. The banana and coconut desserts are island-wide, for all the islanders have a sweet tooth, and rum is another unifier, though the rums vary greatly in type. Wherever the traveller goes in the Caribbean, rum – dark, white or golden – will be there to welcome him.

ATLANTIC OCEAN

DOMINICAN REPUBLIC

PUERTO RICO

VIRGIN ISLANDS

LEEWARD ISLANDS

ANGUILLA

SAINT MARTIN
SINT MAARTEN

BARBUDA

ST CROIX

ST KITTS
NEVIS

ANTIGUA

MONTSERRAT

GUADELOUPE

DOMINICA

MARTINIQUE

ST LUCIA

ST VINCENT

WINDWARD ISLANDS

BARBADOS

ARUBA CURAÇAO

BONAIRE

GRENADA

LESSER ANTILLES

TOBAGO

TRINIDAD

VENEZUELA

# INGREDIENTS AND SPECIALITIES

**ACKEES** Ackees are the fruit of a West African tree, *Blighia sapida*, named in honour of Captain Bligh who introduced it to Jamaica. It is a handsome tree and the fruit with its scarlet shell and shiny black seeds is handsome too. The edible part is the aril, which looks rather like scrambled egg. It is an important part of Jamaica's best-known dish, Salt Codfish and Ackee (page 36). It is available canned and can be found in West Indian food shops.

**ALLSPICE** Allspice is the dried fruit of the pimento tree, a tree native to the West Indies. It adds a flavour similar to a mixture of cloves, cinnamon and nutmeg. It is a common ingredient in many Caribbean dishes, particularly those from Jamaica. It is usually used whole, when it resembles peppercorns, but ground allspice does just as well.

**ANNATTO OIL** A number of Caribbean dishes use annatto oil, *aceite de achiote*, made from the orange-red pulp surrounding the seeds of a small flowering tree, *Bixa orellana*, native to the West Indies and South America. The oil, which has a delicate flavour, is used mostly to colour foods. As it is not easily available here, paprika mixed with corn oil can be used instead.

**COCONUT MILK** Coconut milk is used in the cooking of all the islands in a wide range of recipes. The best available source is pure creamed coconut, which simply needs diluting to the desired consistency using either water or milk according to the richness desired. Otherwise canned coconut milk, sometimes called coconut juice, can be used; or it can be made by simmering desiccated coconut in water which is then sieved and strained.

*Fresh coconut:* Coconuts are nearly always available and it is easy to make coconut milk or cream from them if wished. Pierce two of the eyes in the coconut and drain out the liquid.

This is coconut water and is delicious by itself or with ice, gin, vodka, tequila or rum.

Then bake the coconut in a moderate oven preheated to Gas Mark 6/200°C/400°F for 15 minutes. Put the coconut onto a hard surface and hit it all over with a hammer until the hard shell falls away. With a knife or a screwdriver lever out any bits that do not fall away from the shell. If making coconut milk the brown skin can be left on, as it will not affect the milk. For some recipes, such as salads or sweets, it may be necessary to peel this away using a small, sharp knife.

Chop the coconut into small pieces, put these into a food processor and grate or chop as finely as possible. A little water, or the coconut water, may be added to help the process. Turn the coconut out into a clean, damp cloth and squeeze and twist it, extracting as much liquid as possible. This will be very rich coconut cream. It can be mixed with thinner coconut milk or used by itself.

Put the squeezed-out coconut into a bowl with 300 ml (½ pint) of boiling water and let it stand for 15 minutes. Squeeze out again through the cloth. This is ordinary coconut milk. The process may be repeated once more, letting the coconut stand a little longer.

The average coconut will give 600–750 ml (1–1¼ pints) of coconut milk, depending on the freshness of the coconut.

**PEPPERS AND CHILLIES** Capsicums, members of the huge *Solanaceae* family which includes potatoes, tomatoes and aubergines, are best known here as sweet peppers and hot chillies. They are legion, and so are their names. Native to Mexico and perhaps other parts of tropical America, they have spread all over the world but had already spread to the islands before Columbus even arrived. It is not surprising that their use characterises all island cooking.

Hot Scotch Bonnet, a small, lantern-shaped, bright orange-yellow chilli, is not only very hot but has an enticing flavour. It probably originated in the Yucatán peninsula of Mexico and enjoys the fame of being just about the hottest chilli in North America. I first tasted it in Jamaica as a schoolgirl and never forgot it. I recognized the taste when, years later, I met it in Guatemala as *chile Caballero*, 'gentleman chilli', a tribute to its strength and, I like to think, also to the elegance of its flavour, as many hot chillies simply impart heat and nothing more.

Chillies can irritate the skin, so it is essential to wash your hands with soap and warm water after handling them and to avoid touching your eyes while working with them. Those with sensitive skin might wear rubber gloves.

**PLANTAINS** Plantains, the larger members of the banana family that must be cooked before they can be eaten, are very popular whether used unripe (green), half-ripe (yellow) or ripe (black). The ripe plantains are sweeter but must still be cooked. They can be found in all the islands in many guises, in fact it is hard to imagine Caribbean cooking without them.

**ROOT VEGETABLES** The islands rejoice in a rich variety of root vegetables, most of which originated in tropical regions of the Americas and many of which came with the earliest settlers, the Arawaks, who were good farmers. Identifying them can be quite confusing, but fortunately they can all be used in any recipe suitable for potatoes. With their wide range of subtle flavours they have an enlivening effect on meals, especially when served to accompany Caribbean main dishes of fish, poultry or meat.

The principal ones to look out for are the sweet potatoes, which is where confusion begins as the Louisiana yam – with moist orange yellow flesh and a brown skin – is not a yam at all, but a variety of sweet potato. The preferred sweet potato of the islands is the boniato, which has much drier white flesh and a pink or white skin.

Another large group of plants with edible

tubers are the taros and malangas, very closely related. They are members of the *Arum* family and have been cultivated for more than 2,000 years, which might go some way to explaining why there are so many of them and why they have so many names. Among other things, some of them give us the green leaves used to make Callaloo soup (page 24). The inedible members of this family grow in our gardens, the arthuriums, philodendrons and calla lilies. The edible tubers are most likely to be met with as coco, eddoe, malanga, dasheen, tannia and yautía. They come in a wide range of sizes, have rough brown skin and flesh that ranges from white to yellow, grey-white and purple.

Another large group are the yams – edible tubers of plants of the *Dioscorea* family. They come in a great variety of sizes and shapes, though not with so many names. Most of them are the size of a large potato and have white or yellow flesh with a pleasant nut-like flavour, and a texture rather like potatoes.

Finally there is cassava, *Manihot utilissima*, known also as manioc, yuca and gari. The roots are long – up to 25 cm (10 inches) – with a hairy, brown, rather bark-like skin. They can be bought in this form and can be peeled and boiled or fried. Tapioca is made from this plant and cassava meal can be bought packaged, ready to use in recipes. The flavour is nutty and delicate. *Cassareep*, a flavouring originating in Guyana and popular in Trinidad, is made from cassava.

For the most part these root vegetables can be used interchangably, especially when getting to know them.

**SALT CODFISH** Sa¹ᵗ ᵤtish has always been important in th⸍ ᵢnes of Portugal and Spain, discoverers of the islands, and though the waters teem with fish, salt codfish is still a favourite with island cooks. It is used in fish cakes and in Jamaica's most famous dish, Salt Codfish and Ackee (page 36). It can be found in some delicatessens and fish markets.

# BASIC RECIPE

## SOFRITO

Makes about 350 ml (12 fl oz)

Preparation time: 40 minutes + 30 minutes cooking

*50 g (2 oz) smoked streaky bacon or salt pork, rind removed, diced finely*

*1 tablespoon corn oil, mixed with 1 tablespoon paprika*

*2 onions, chopped finely*

*4 garlic cloves, chopped*

*2 green peppers, cored, de-seeded and chopped finely*

*125 g (4 oz) lean, boneless ham, diced*

*500 g (1 lb) tomatoes, skinned, de-seeded and chopped*

*2 tablespoons chopped fresh coriander*

*½ teaspoon dried oregano*

*salt and pepper*

*The cooking of the Spanish-speaking islands uses that favourite Spanish cooking base, the* sofrito, *considerably changed from the original recipe brought by Spanish settlers. It can be made ahead and refrigerated for up to a week, ready to be used when needed.*

In a heavy frying pan, gently fry the bacon or pork pieces over a moderate heat until they have given up all their fat and are crisp and brown. Lift out with a slotted spoon and reserve.

Add the paprika oil to the pan with the onions, garlic and green peppers and gently fry over a moderate heat for about 5 minutes until the vegetables are soft. Add the ham, tomatoes, coriander, oregano, the reserved bacon or pork and salt and pepper and simmer, covered, over a low heat for 30 minutes, stirring from time to time to prevent the mixture from sticking.

Leave to cool. Pour into glass jars, cover and refrigerate until needed. Use as directed in recipes.

*Variation*: This method is often used in Cuba. Combine all the ingredients in a food processor and reduce to a coarse purée. Pour into a saucepan, bring to the boil and simmer over a very low heat for 15–20 minutes, stirring occasionally. Cool, pour into jars, refrigerate and use as needed.

# APPETISERS

## BANANA CHIPS

Preparation time: 5 minutes + 30 minutes soaking + 5 minutes cooking

*semi-green bananas*

*oil for deep-frying*

*salt*

*In St Kitts green (unripe) bananas cooked this way are a favourite nibble to accompany drinks. On the island of St Vincent white sweet potatoes (boniatos) are cooked in the same way. Many of the other islands use green plantains. Allow about one banana per person.*

Peel the bananas and slice crossways as thinly as possible. Drop into salted iced water and leave them to soak for 30 minutes. Drain and dry on kitchen paper.

Deep-fry the banana slices for 3–4 minutes in oil heated to 190°C/375°F on a frying thermometer, until lightly browned. Drain on kitchen paper, sprinkle with salt and serve as an accompaniment to drinks.

## SURULLITOS

Corn and cheese sticks                                   Makes 24

Preparation time: 5 minutes + 30 minutes cooking

*600 ml (1 pint) water*

*1 teaspoon salt*

*175 g (6 oz) yellow maize meal*

*125 g (4 oz) grated Edam or mild Cheddar cheese*

*oil for shallow-frying*

*These corn sticks from Puerto Rico, served warm or at room temperature, make a robust accompaniment to drinks. They can also be served as a hot bread to accompany a main course.*

Bring the water and salt to a boil in a saucepan and pour in the maize meal in a thin, steady stream. Cook for about 4 minutes over a moderate heat, stirring constantly with a wooden spoon, until the mixture is thick and smooth. Remove from the heat and beat in the cheese, mixing well. Leave to cool.

Take out dessertspoonfuls of the mixture and make into small logs 7 cm (3 inches) long. Heat a little oil in a large, heavy frying pan and fry the corn sticks for about 5 minutes in batches of 4–6 over a moderate heat, until golden brown all over. Lift out with a spatula onto kitchen paper to drain.

## BOMBAS DE CAMARONES Y PAPAS

Prawn and potato balls                    Makes about 30

Preparation time: 30 minutes + 15 minutes cooking + 30 minutes chilling

*500 g (1 lb) potatoes, peeled and quartered*

*40 g (1½ oz) butter*

*1 egg, beaten lightly, plus 2 egg yolks*

*50 g (2 oz) Edam or Cheddar cheese, grated*

*1 tablespoon finely chopped fresh parsley*

*1 onion, chopped finely*

*500 g (1 lb) peeled prawns, thawed if frozen, chopped coarsely*

*plain flour for rolling*

*50 g (2 oz) dry breadcrumbs*

*oil for frying*

*salt and pepper*

*Crabes Farcis (Stuffed crabs)*
*Bombas de Camarones y Papas (Prawn and potato balls)*

*These are useful as a hot appetiser that can be made ahead of time and kept, refrigerated, until ready to cook; then they can be quickly deep-fried and served on cocktail sticks to accompany drinks. They are very flexible as they can be made larger to serve with a tomato or other sauce as a first course, or simply garnished with lemon slices. They are popular in the Dominican Republic.*

Put the potatoes into a saucepan with cold salted water to cover and boil until tender. Drain very well and mash with 25 g (1 oz) of the butter, the egg yolks, cheese, parsley and salt and pepper to taste. Set aside.

Heat the remaining butter in a small frying pan and gently fry the onion until it is soft but not brown. Leave to cool.

Stir the prawns into the onions and mix well. Combine the prawn mixture with the mashed potato and form into small balls about 1 cm (½ inch) in diameter. Place on a baking sheet lined with greaseproof paper and refrigerate for 30 minutes or until ready to cook.

Roll the balls lightly in flour, dip in the beaten egg and then coat with the breadcrumbs.

Pour enough oil into a frying pan to reach a depth of 5 cm (2 inches) and when it is hot but not smoking – 190°C/375°F on a frying thermometer – fry the prawn balls in batches until golden brown all over. Drain on kitchen paper and serve at once.

# CRABES FARCIS

Preparation time: 25 minutes + 30 minutes cooking

*500 g (1 lb) fresh or canned brown and/or white crabmeat*

*75 g (3 oz) fresh white breadcrumbs*

*1 small chilli, de-seeded and chopped finely*

*3 tablespoons snipped chives*

*2 tablespoons finely chopped fresh parsley*

*2 garlic cloves, crushed*

*1 tablespoon lime or lemon juice*

*¼ teaspoon ground allspice*

*3 tablespoons dark rum, preferably Martinique or Guadeloupe rhum vieux*

*25 g (1 oz) butter*

*salt and pepper*

*The violet-coloured land crabs of the islands would be used in this dish, but our crabs do just as well. Scallop shells can be used instead of small crab shells with equally appetising results. Recipes for stuffed crabs vary from island to island, mostly in the seasonings used. This one comes from Martinique and Guadeloupe.*

Preheat the oven to Gas Mark 4/180°C/350°F.

In a bowl combine the crabmeat with 50 g (2 oz) of the breadcrumbs and mash until smooth. Add all the remaining ingredients, except the remaining breadcrumbs and the butter, mixing well. Alternatively, mix the ingredients in a food processor.

Lightly butter six scallop shells and stuff with the crab mixture. Sprinkle with the remaining breadcrumbs and dot with the rest of the butter. Place the shells on a baking sheet and bake in the oven for about 30 minutes, until lightly browned.

# SAVOURY FRITTERS

Makes 20–24

Preparation time: 5 minutes + 1 hour standing + 15 minutes cooking

### For the batter:

125 g (4 oz) plain flour

1½ teaspoons baking powder

½ teaspoon salt

4 eggs

2 teaspoons melted butter

2 teaspoons corn or groundnut oil

2 teaspoons white rum

### For the fritters:

125 g (4 oz) cooked chicken, coarsely chopped peeled prawns, cooked chopped lobster, cooked chopped crabmeat or sweetcorn kernels

groundnut or corn oil for deep-frying

*These fried morsels, whether they are called fritters in the English-speaking islands,* beignets *in the French-speaking islands, or* frituras *in the Spanish-speaking islands, are extremely popular island-wide as an accompaniment to drinks or as a first course. They invite the cook to use imagination by adding chopped chives, a little chopped chilli or any other seasoning to the batter, or by using chopped crabmeat, lobster or conch, if it is available, as the filling. Vegetarians can use almost any cooked vegetable. Indeed there is no limit to the variations that the island cooks play on the fritter theme.*

Sift the flour, baking powder and salt into a bowl. Make a well in the centre and break in the eggs. Add the butter, oil and rum and beat until the batter is smooth. Leave to stand at room temperature for 1 hour.

Mix the batter with either the chicken, prawns, lobster, crabmeat or sweetcorn. Drop tablespoons of the mixture into oil heated to 190°C/375°F on a frying thermometer. Deep-fry for 6–8 minutes until golden brown all over. Drain on kitchen paper and serve.

*Note*: If liked, shallow-fry the fritters. Heat 5 cm (2 inches) of oil in a frying pan until a teaspoon of the batter sizzles on contact and then fry the fritters until golden brown on both sides.

# CAVEACHED FISH

Pickled fish                    Serves 8 as a first course or 4 as a main course

Preparation time: 15 minutes + 35 minutes cooking + 2 hours if chilling

2 green peppers, cored, de-seeded and sliced

2 onions, sliced thinly

2 carrots, sliced thinly

1 bay leaf

2.5 cm (1-inch) piece of fresh root ginger, peeled and chopped finely

8 black peppercorns

a pinch of ground mace

¼ teaspoon chilli powder

450 ml (¾ pint) water

6 tablespoons olive oil

125 ml (4 fl oz) light malt or cider vinegar

1 kg (2 lb) red snapper fillets, or any firm-fleshed white fish

salt

**To garnish:**

green olives

red pepper strips

*Jamaica was once a Spanish island and this Jamaican dish derives from Spanish cooking, its original name Pescado en Escabeche (Pickled Fish). In the course of time* escabeche *has changed into* caveached *or sometimes* escovitch *in Jamaica. Though traditionally a first course it is sometimes served as a main course. In Puerto Rico it turns up with its Spanish name intact. Jamaican cooks have given the dish their special touch with the addition of green peppers, ginger and mace.*

In a large saucepan combine the peppers, onions, carrots, bay leaf, ginger, peppercorns, mace, chilli powder and water and add a little salt. Simmer, covered, for 30 minutes. Add 2 tablespooons of the oil and the vinegar and simmer for 2 minutes longer. Set aside and keep hot if wished.

Heat the remaining oil in a large, heavy frying pan and gently fry the fish fillets, in batches so as not to crowd the pan, for 2–3 minutes on each side. Transfer the fillets as they are cooked to a shallow serving dish. Pour the hot sauce over the fish and serve hot, or chill the dish in the refrigerator and serve cold, garnished with olives and pepper strips.

# SOUPS

## GROUNDNUT SOUP

Serves 4–6

Preparation time: 15 minutes + 20 minutes cooking

*2 teaspoons groundnut or corn oil*

*1 onion, chopped finely*

*125 g (4 oz) roasted peanuts, ground finely*

*1 small red or green chilli, de-seeded and chopped*

*1 litre (1¾ pints) chicken stock*

*142 ml (¼ pint) carton of single cream*

*1 teaspoon angostura bitters*

*salt and pepper*

*2 tablespoons chopped chives, to garnish*

*Peanuts, sometimes called groundnuts, have a dual origin. They were originally cultivated by Guaraní Indians in Brazil and also, at roughly the same time, thousands of years ago, in West Africa, though this was of a different genus. It is not surprising to find that groundnut soup is a favourite all over the Caribbean and the Americas. This particular one is popular in St Kitts.*

Heat the oil in a small frying pan and gently fry the onion until it is soft. Lift out the onion with a slotted spoon and transfer to a food processor, discarding any oil. Add the peanuts, chilli and a little of the stock to the food processor and blend to a smooth purée.

Transfer the mixture to a saucepan and stir in the rest of the stock. Season with salt and pepper, bring to a simmer and cook, covered, for 15 minutes.

Stir the cream into the soup and cook just long enough to heat through. Stir in the angostura bitters and serve in soup bowls, garnished with the chives.

## CHILLED CUCUMBER SOUP

Serves 6

Preparation time: 15 minutes + 20 minutes cooking + 3–4 hours chilling

*750 g (1½ lb) cucumbers, peeled, de-seeded and chopped*

*1 onion, chopped*

*This delicious soup from Barbados is ideal for hot weather, light and refreshing in contrast with some of the more robust Caribbean soups. It can be made ahead of time as it needs thorough chilling, useful when planning a summer dinner party.*

|  |
|---|
| 1.2 litres (2 pints) chicken stock |
| 1 tablespoon arrowroot |
| 250 ml (8 fl oz) single cream |
| salt and white pepper |
| 2 tablespoons chopped fresh chives, parsley or mint, to garnish |

Combine the cucumbers, onion and chicken stock in a large saucepan. Bring to a simmer, cover and cook over a low heat for 15 minutes. Leave to cool.

Strain the soup through a sieve set over a bowl. Transfer the mixture left in the sieve to a food processor with a little of the liquid and reduce to a purée. Return the purée and the rest of the liquid to the saucepan and stir. Season generously with salt and pepper.

Mix the arrowroot with a little cold water and stir into the soup. Cook for a minute or two, just long enough to lightly thicken the soup. Remove from the heat, stir in the cream and chill for several hours in the refrigerator. Serve garnished with the chives, parsley or mint.

## CREAM OF PUMPKIN SOUP

Serves 6–8

Preparation time: 20 minutes + 55 minutes cooking + 2 hours if chilling

|  |
|---|
| 25 g (1 oz) butter |
| 1 large onion, chopped coarsely |
| 1.25 kg (3 lb) pumpkin, peeled, de-seeded and cubed |
| 1.2 litres (2 pints) chicken stock |
| 1 teaspoon ground coriander |
| 1 small red chilli, de-seeded and chopped |
| 250 ml (8 fl oz) single cream |
| salt and pepper |

*The full, rich flavour of pumpkin comes through clearly in this simple Jamaican version of pumpkin soup. Delicious hot, it is also very good chilled.*

Melt the butter in a large, heavy saucepan and gently fry the onion over a low heat until it is soft. Add the pumpkin, chicken stock, coriander and chilli. Bring to a simmer, cover and cook over a low heat for about 45 minutes, stirring once or twice, until the pumpkin disintegrates.

Strain the soup through a sieve set over a bowl. Return the liquid to the saucepan. Purée the mixture left in the sieve in a food processor. Do not overblend as the soup should retain some texture. Add to the saucepan, stir in the cream and season to taste with salt and pepper. Reheat gently. Serve in soup bowls. If serving cold, chill in the refrigerator for at least 2 hours.

# PRAWN AND SWEETCORN SOUP

Preparation time: 15 minutes + 45 minutes cooking

25 g (1 oz) butter

1 onion, chopped finely

1 garlic clove, chopped

2 extra large tomatoes, skinned, de-seeded and chopped

1 bay leaf

450 ml (¾ pint) fish stock

6 small new potatoes

750 ml (1¼ pints) milk

375 g (12 oz) sweetcorn kernels, thawed if frozen

2 large egg yolks (size 1 or 2), beaten lightly

375–500 g (12 oz–1 lb) peeled prawns, thawed if frozen

salt and pepper

*This sturdy, yet elegant soup is a fine example of Cuban cooking, which combines the best of both worlds, Old and New. Strongly influenced by Spanish cooking and with skilfully introduced New World foods like potatoes, tomatoes and corn, the soup is filling enough to make a main course for a lunch served with a green salad. Purists serve the sweetcorn on the cob cut into 2.5 cm (1-inch) slices. A convenient variation is to add frozen or canned sweetcorn kernels, as in this version.*

Melt the butter in a large saucepan. Add the onion and garlic and fry gently over a moderate heat until the onion is soft. Add the tomatoes, bay leaf and fish stock, cover and cook for 15 minutes.

Strain the soup through a sieve set over a bowl, pushing down hard on the vegetables to extract all the flavours. Discard the mixture left in the sieve. Return the liquid to the saucepan and add the potatoes. Cook, covered, for about 15 minutes, until the potatoes are almost tender.

Stir the milk and sweetcorn into the soup and simmer for 5 minutes longer over a low heat. Season to taste with salt and pepper.

Whisk 4 tablespoons of the hot soup into the beaten egg yolks and then stir the mixture back into the soup over a low heat to thicken it lightly. Add the prawns and cook for about 1 minute, just long enough to heat them through: they toughen easily if overcooked. Serve in soup bowls, making sure there is a potato in each bowl.

# CALLALOO

Preparation time: 20 minutes + 20 minutes cooking

25 g (1 oz) butter

125 g (4 oz) bacon or lean salt pork, cut into 1 cm (½-inch) cubes

1 onion, chopped finely

1 garlic clove, chopped

500 g (1 lb) callaloo leaves, pak choi, choi sam, spinach or green part of Swiss chard, shredded

a sprig of fresh thyme or ½ teaspoon dried thyme

1.5 litres (2½ pints) chicken stock or water

125 ml (4 fl oz) coconut milk (page 10)

250 g (8 oz) fresh or canned brown and/or white crabmeat

250 g (8 oz) okra, trimmed and sliced

West Indian hot pepper sauce or Tabasco sauce, to taste

salt and pepper

This is perhaps the most famous of all the island soups, with many islands having their own slightly differing versions. This one is from Trinidad. Even the green leaves used in the soup can come from one of two distinct types of plant. The elephant ear leaves of a group of tropical plants with edible tubers called taro are the kind usually used. These tubers, also popular in island cooking, may be called coco, dasheen, tannia, or yautía among others. The other leafy green vegetable that is often used in the soup is Chinese spinach. All is not lost if neither of these leafy vegetables is available as spinach or the green part of Swiss chard have a similar texture and flavour. The soup is hearty enough to be served as a main course.

In a large, heavy saucepan melt the butter and fry the bacon or pork cubes for 2–3 minutes. Add the onion and garlic and gently fry until the vegetables are soft. Add the greens and stir to mix. Add the thyme. Pour in the stock or water and coconut milk and simmer for 10 minutes, or until the greens are tender.

Add the crabmeat and okra to the pan and simmer for 10 minutes longer. Season to taste with salt, pepper and hot pepper or Tabasco sauce. Serve in large soup plates.

*Callaloo*
*Prawn and Sweetcorn*
*Soup*

# SOUPE AU POISSON

Preparation time: 30 minutes + 35 minutes cooking

2 tablespoons olive oil

1 large onion, chopped finely

3 spring onions, white and green parts, chopped

2 garlic cloves, crushed

500 g (1 lb) tomatoes, skinned, de-seeded and chopped

1 tablespoon paprika

2.25 litres (4 pints) water

1.25 kg (3 lb) whole fish, heads removed, cut into 5 cm (2-inch) pieces, e.g. sea bass or red snapper, or any white-fleshed fish

2 small whole red or green chillies

a good pinch of ground allspice

1 bay leaf

500 g (1 lb) potatoes, peeled and sliced

*Fish soups are popular in the islands, especially in the French ones. This version is from Martinique and Guadeloupe. Favourite fish used are sea bass, striped bass, bream and snapper. The main thing is to avoid oily fish. Some cooks include a little dry white wine with the cooking liquid, others add 125 ml (4 fl oz) of Pernod to the soup with the fish towards the end of cooking, while still others substitute 250 ml (8 fl oz) of coconut milk for part of the water. Cooks can please themselves what they choose.*

Heat the oil in a large saucepan and gently fry the onion, spring onions and garlic until soft. Add the tomatoes and cook 3–4 minutes longer to blend the flavours. Add the paprika and stir to mix. Add all the remaining ingredients, bring to a simmer and cook, uncovered, over a low heat for 30 minutes.

Lift out the fish and, when it is cool enough to handle, remove and discard any skin and bones. Set the fish aside.

Strain the soup through a sieve set over a bowl, pressing down hard on the vegetables to extract all the flavours. Discard the vegetables and return the liquid to the saucepan. Add the fish and cook just long enough to heat it through. Serve in soup bowls, accompanied by crusty bread.

# RED PEA SOUP

Preparation time: overnight soaking + 10–15 minutes + 2¼–3¼ hours cooking

500 g (1 lb) red kidney beans

275 ml (9 fl oz) Sofrito (page 14)

a sprig of fresh thyme or ½ teaspoon dried thyme

900 ml (1½ pints) beef or chicken stock

salt and pepper

West Indian hot pepper sauce or Tabasco sauce, to serve

*Bean soups of various kinds are popular throughout the islands, with classic recipes coming from Cuba, Jamaica, Trinidad and Puerto Rico. The type of beans usually used are black and red kidney beans. The red peas in this Jamaican soup are really beans. They are not identical to red kidney beans but are a very close relative, differing so slightly that red kidney beans can be used. Pigeon peas, which are beans of African origin variously called* gunga *peas,* gandules *and* arhar dahl, *are also used in soups. Recipes for these are very different from kidney beans, which come originally from Mexico.*

Put the beans into a large saucepan with cold water to cover by about 5 cm (2 inches) and leave to soak overnight.

When ready to cook, drain and discard the soaking water. Rinse the beans and return to the saucepan with the Sofrito, thyme and stock. Bring to the boil and boil rapidly for 10 minutes. Reduce the heat to a simmer, cover and cook over a low heat, stirring from time to time to prevent the beans from sticking, for 2–3 hours, or until the beans are very tender and can be mashed against the side of the saucepan with a wooden spoon. (The time will depend on the freshness of the beans.) If they seem to be drying out during cooking, add a little more hot stock or water.

Drain the cooked beans through a sieve set over a bowl. Measure the liquid and add more stock to bring the quantity up to 1.2 litres (2 pints) if necessary. Purée the beans in batches in a food processor, adding a little of the measured liquid. Do not overblend: the soup should retain some texture. Scrape the bean purée into the saucepan, add the remaining stock, stir and add seasoning to taste.

Simmer gently for 15 minutes longer. Serve in soup bowls, accompanied by West Indian hot pepper sauce or Tabasco sauce.

*Variation*: To make Sopa de Frijol Negro (Black bean soup) from Cuba, make the soup with black kidney beans in exactly the same way as Red Pea Soup but use ¼ teaspoon of ground cumin instead of the thyme. Add 2 tablespoons of light malt vinegar before simmering the puréed soup and garnish with chopped onion.

# CONSOMMÉ À L'ORANGE

Serves 6

Preparation time: 10 minutes + 15 minutes cooking + 3–4 hours chilling

900 ml (1½ pints) rich, clarified chicken stock

450 ml (¾ pint) orange juice, strained

a good pinch of ground allspice

salt and white pepper

1 orange, pips removed, sliced very thinly, to garnish

*This soup from Haiti shows the persistence, in its flavourful elegance, of French culinary techniques. A lovely hot weather soup, it is even better in its jellied version – a variation from the island of Grenada.*

If necessary, strain the stock through a sieve lined with muslin to ensure that it is completely fat free.

In a saucepan combine the chicken stock with the orange juice and allspice, and salt and pepper to taste. Bring to a simmer, cover and cook over a very low heat for 15 minutes.

Strain the soup through a sieve lined with muslin and chill thoroughly in the refrigerator, preferably for 3–4 hours. Serve garnished with the orange slices.

*Variation*: For Jellied Consommé à l'Orange, pour 125 ml (4 fl oz) of cold water into a small bowl. Sprinkle two 57 g (2 oz) sachets of gelatine over the water to soften. Add to the strained soup before it is chilled and simmer, stirring, just long enough to dissolve the gelatine. Chill for about 2 hours in the refrigerator until set. Break up the jelly with a fork and serve garnished with the orange slices.

*Red Pea Soup*
*Consommé à l'Orange*

# FISH AND SHELLFISH

## CURRIED FISH

Serves 4–6

Preparation time: 15 minutes + 15–20 minutes cooking

50 g (2 oz) butter

2 onions, chopped finely

1 tablespoon mild or hot curry powder, to taste

1 tablespoon plain flour

300 ml (½ pint) coconut milk (page 10) or single cream

750 g (1½ lb) fillets of any white-fleshed fish, skinned and cut into 5 cm (2-inch) pieces, e.g. cod, haddock, plaice or sole

1 tablespoon lime juice

salt and pepper

*Flying fish are the great speciality in this dish from Barbados, but fillets of any white fish can be used as a good substitute.*

Melt the butter in a frying pan and gently fry the onions until they are soft. Stir in the curry powder and gently fry for 2–3 minutes longer. Add the flour, stir to mix and cook for 1–2 minutes. Gradually stir in the coconut milk or single cream and simmer until the sauce is thickened. If it is too thick, thin with a little milk or water. Season with salt and pepper.

Arrange the fish in a flameproof casserole and sprinkle with the lime juice. Pour the curry sauce over it and simmer for 10 minutes, or just long enough to cook the fish. Serve with rice.

## PRAWN CURRY

Serves 4–6

Preparation time: 10–15 minutes + 45 minutes cooking

1½ tablespoons mild or hot curry powder, to taste

½ teaspoon chilli powder

1 bay leaf, crumbled

3 tablespoons corn, groundnut or vegetable oil

40 g (1½ oz) butter

2 large onions, chopped finely

2 garlic cloves, crushed

*Curry was introduced to Trinidad by migrant Hindu workers from India. Cooks had their favourite spice mixtures which they ground just before cooking, and many island cooks still do this. However there are many excellent curry powders available today, perfectly acceptable for this prawn curry. Choose the one with the preferred level of hotness, as some can be very hot indeed.*

In a small bowl combine the curry powder, chilli powder and bay leaf and set aside.

Heat the oil and butter in a large frying pan and gently fry the onions until lightly browned.

| | Add the garlic, ginger and curry powder mixture and gently fry, stirring, for 2 minutes. Add the tomatoes and lime or lemon juice and season to taste with salt. Cover and cook, stirring occasionally, over a very low heat for 30 minutes. The mixture should be thick. If necessary, add a little chicken stock or water. |
|---|---|

*2.5 cm (1-inch) piece of fresh root ginger, peeled and chopped finely*

*500 g (1 lb) tomatoes, skinned and chopped*

*2 tablespoons lime or lemon juice*

*1 kg (2 lb) peeled prawns, thawed if frozen*

*salt*

Add the garlic, ginger and curry powder mixture and gently fry, stirring, for 2 minutes. Add the tomatoes and lime or lemon juice and season to taste with salt. Cover and cook, stirring occasionally, over a very low heat for 30 minutes. The mixture should be thick. If necessary, add a little chicken stock or water.

Add the prawns and cook for about 1 minute, or just long enough to heat them through: they toughen quickly if overcooked. Serve with rice and mango chutney.

# PARGO CON SALSA DE AGUACATE

Sea bass with avocado sauce                                      Serves 4

Preparation time: 20 minutes + about 50 minutes cooking

**For the fish:**

*50 g (2 oz) butter*

*1.25–1.75 kg (3–4 lb) whole sea bass, head and tail left on*

*2 tablespoons lime or lemon juice*

*4 tablespoons dry white wine*

*salt and pepper*

**For the sauce:**

*2 large ripe avocados, peeled, stoned and mashed*

*1 tablespoon lime juice*

*3 tablespoons vegetable oil*

*1 tablespoon finely chopped onion (optional)*

*salt and pepper*

**To garnish:**

*lettuce leaves*

*lemon or lime slices*

*fresh parsley sprigs*

*This variation of Pargo con Cilantro (Sea bass with coriander, page 35) makes a wonderful summer dish served cold with an avocado sauce.*

Preheat the oven to Gas Mark 7/220°C/425°F.

Lightly butter a piece of foil large enough to wrap the fish. Place the fish on the foil. Chop the rest of the butter and dot the fish with it. Sprinkle with the lime or lemon juice, pour the wine over and season with salt and pepper. Fold the foil over the fish and turn the ends up to seal.

Bake the fish in the oven, allowing 10 minutes for each 2.5 cm (1 inch) of fish measured at the thickest part. Transfer to a platter and leave to cool.

Meanwhile, make the sauce. In a bowl combine the avocados, lime juice, vegetable oil, onion, if using, and salt and pepper to taste. Whisk to the consistency of mayonnaise.

Remove the skin from the upturned side of the fish and mask with the sauce. Garnish the platter with lettuce leaves, lemon or lime slices and parsley and serve any extra sauce separately.

# SALMOREJO DE JUEYES

Crab stew                                              Serves 6

Preparation time: 15 minutes + 20 minutes cooking

750 g (1½ lb) fresh or
canned brown and/or white
crabmeat

2 garlic cloves, crushed

1 onion, chopped finely

2 red peppers, cored de-
seeded and chopped finely

1 small red chilli, de-seeded
and chopped

4 tablespoons olive oil

4 tablespoons lime or lemon
juice

4 tablespoons cider or light
malt vinegar

12 green olives, pitted and
halved

salt and pepper

Land crabs are a Puerto Rican speciality but are not
generally available. They are more strongly
flavoured than sea crabs, although these are a very
good substitute. Salmorejo is a Spanish sauce
made of vinegar, oil and salt and pepper. In Puerto
Rico achiote (annatto) oil made with olive oil is
often used, but it is not essential.

Combine all the ingredients in a saucepan.
Bring to the boil, cover and simmer over a very
low heat for 20 minutes.
    Serve the stew with rice and Fried Ripe
Plantains (page 70).

Pescado Frito en Salsa de
Coco (Fried fish in coconut
sauce)

*Arroz con Camarones*
*(Prawns and rice)*

*Salmorejo de Jueyes*
*(Crab stew)*

# ARROZ CON CAMARONES

Preparation time: 15–20 minutes + 40 minutes cooking

4 tablespoons olive, corn or
groundnut oil

2 onions, chopped finely

2 garlic cloves, chopped

1 large red pepper, cored,
de-seeded and chopped
coarsely

500 g (1 lb) long-grain rice

1 litre (1¾ pints) chicken
stock

500 g (1 lb) tomatoes,
skinned, de-seeded and
chopped

1–2 small red chillies, de-
seeded and chopped
(optional)

2 tablespoons chopped fresh
coriander

1 tablespoon paprika

500 g (1 lb) peeled prawns,
thawed if frozen

salt and pepper

*The Dominican Republic, which shares its island
with Haiti, is famed in the Caribbean for its good
cooking. The strong Spanish influence in this dish
is balanced by the use of New World ingredients –
tomatoes, peppers and chillies. Some cooks use
achiote (annatto) oil to colour and flavour. Others
use paprika, as in this version.*

Heat the oil in a large frying pan that has a lid.
Gently fry the onions, garlic and red pepper
until soft. Add the rice, stir and cook over a
moderate heat until the rice has absorbed all
the oil, taking care not to let it brown. Add the
chicken stock, tomatoes, chillies, coriander and
paprika, and salt and pepper to taste. Bring to a
simmer, cover and cook over a low heat until
the rice is tender and all the liquid has been
absorbed.

　Add the prawns to the frying pan and stir
gently to mix. Cook only long enough to heat
the prawns through: they toughen easily.

# PESCADO FRITO EN SALSA DE COCO

Preparation time: 20 minutes + 1 hour marinating + 25 minutes
cooking

**For the fish:**

4 garlic cloves, crushed

2 teaspoons salt

½ teaspoon dried oregano

¼ teaspoon pepper

*The Dominican Republic is noted for the excellence
of its cuisine, full of originality as this fish dish
shows.*

In a small bowl mix together the garlic, salt,
oregano, pepper and lime juice. Arrange the
fish fillets in a shallow dish and cover with the

4 tablespoons lime juice

1 kg (2 lb) fillets of any white-fleshed fish, e.g. cod, haddock, plaice or sole

plain flour for sprinkling

125 ml (4 fl oz) groundnut oil

**For the sauce:**

1 small leek, chopped

1 small green chilli, de-seeded and chopped

1 bay leaf

1 tablespoon chopped fresh parsley

1 tablespoon chopped fresh coriander

2 tablespoons tomato purée

350 ml (12 fl oz) coconut milk (page 10)

salt and pepper

garlic mixture. Leave for 1 hour in a cool place or in the refrigerator, turning once or twice.

Lift out the fish and gently scrape off and reserve the marinade. Sprinkle with flour, shaking to remove the excess. Heat the oil in a heavy frying pan and fry the fillets, in batches if necessary, until golden: 2–3 minutes on each side, depending on the thickness of the fish. Be careful not to overcook. Keep the fish warm while making the sauce.

Discard all but 2 tablespoons of the oil in the frying pan. Reheat the oil and gently fry the leek and chilli until the leek is soft. Add the reserved marinade, the bay leaf, parsley, coriander and tomato purée. Stir to mix and cook for 1–2 minutes. Stir in the coconut milk, taste for seasoning and add salt and pepper if necessary. Discard the bay leaf. Heat the sauce through but do not let it boil as it separates easily.

Pour the hot sauce over the fish. Serve with rice or root vegetables (page 12).

## PARGO CON CILANTRO

Sea bass with coriander                                    Serves 4

Preparation time: 20 minutes + about 50 minutes cooking

50 g (2 oz) butter

1.25–1.75 kg (3–4 lb) whole sea bass, head and tail left on

1 onion, sliced thinly

1 tomato, skinned and chopped

1 garlic clove, chopped

3 tablespoons finely chopped fresh coriander

2 tablespoons lime or lemon juice

*Sea bass is an excellent substitute for the Caribbean pargo usually used in this Cuban dish, though any whole white-fleshed fish could be used. A simple way to check the timing for the fish is to measure the depth of the fish at its thickest part and then to cook it for 10 minutes per 2.5 cm (1 inch).*

Preheat the oven to Gas Mark 7/220°C/425°F.

Lightly butter a piece of foil large enough to wrap the whole fish. Place the fish on the foil. Chop the rest of the butter and dot the fish with it. Arrange the onion, tomato, garlic and coriander on the fish and sprinkle with the lime or lemon juice. Pour the wine over the fish and season with salt and pepper. Fold the foil over

4 tablespoons dry white
wine

salt and pepper

the fish and turn the ends up to seal.

Bake the fish in the oven for about 50 minutes, depending on its thickness. Serve with rice.

## SALT CODFISH AND ACKEE

Preparation time: about 2 hours soaking + 30 minutes + 40 minutes cooking

500 g (1 lb) salt codfish

25 g (1 oz) butter

4 bacon rashers

1 onion, chopped finely

1 green pepper, cored, de-
seeded and chopped

4 spring onions, white and
green parts, chopped

1 small chilli, de-seeded and
chopped

3 tomatoes, skinned, de-
seeded and chopped

a sprig of fresh thyme or ¼
teaspoon dried thyme

625 g (1¼ lb) can of
ackees, drained

pepper

1 tomato, cut into 8
wedges, to garnish

*This is Jamaica's most famous dish. It is the ackees that make it so special. This fruit has a delicate flavour that balances well with the more robust taste of salt codfish.*

Put the salt codfish in a bowl with water to cover and soak for 2 hours, changing the water two or three times.

Drain the fish and put it into a saucepan with cold water to cover. Simmer, covered, over a moderate heat for 15–20 minutes, until the fish is tender. Drain, remove any skin and bones, flake the flesh and set aside.

Melt the butter in a frying pan and fry the bacon until crisp. Lift out of the pan, drain on kitchen paper and crumble. Set aside.

In the fat remaining in the pan, gently fry the onion, green pepper and spring onions until soft and very lightly browned. Add the chilli, chopped tomatoes, thyme and pepper to taste and cook for about 5 minutes or until the mixture is well blended.

Add the fish and ackees to the frying pan and heat through. Transfer to a heated dish, sprinkle over the crumbled bacon and garnish with the tomato wedges.

*Pargo con Cilantro (Sea
bass with coriander)
Salt Codfish and Ackee*

# KESHY YENA COE CABARON

Stuffed cheese with prawn filling                                    Serves 6–8

Preparation time: 45 minutes + 1 hour soaking + 30 minutes cooking

2 halves of Edam cheese, weighing 1.75 kg (4 lb) in total

40 g (1½ oz) butter

1 tablespoon corn, groundnut or vegetable oil

1 large onion, chopped finely

500 g (1 lb) tomatoes, skinned, de-seeded and chopped

¼ teaspoon chilli powder

50 g (2 oz) fresh breadcrumbs

2 tablespoons seedless raisins

2 tablespoons sweet gherkin pickle or pickled cucumbers, chopped finely

3 tablespoons finely chopped black olives

750 g (1½ lb) peeled prawns, thawed if frozen, chopped

2 eggs, beaten well

salt and pepper

This dish has a most entertaining origin. It began in the Dutch island of Curaçao, when cooks found an imaginative use for Dutch Edam cheese and called it Keshy Yena in the local island language, Papiamento. This entertaining language is a mixture of Spanish, Portuguese, English, Dutch and African. Dutch and German coffee men going to the States of Chiapas and Yucatán in Mexico took the recipe with them. It changed·a little as migrating recipes are apt to do and reverted to the name it would always have had in Spanish – Queso (cheese) Relleno (stuffed). It is a wonderful dish for a lunch or dinner party. In Curaçao it is made with a whole cheese, but two halves do just as well.

Peel the red wax covering from the cheese halves. Scoop out the cheese inside the halves, leaving 1 cm (½-inch) shells. Put the cheese shells into a large bowl, cover with water and soak for an hour. Grate the scooped-out cheese and set aside 250 g (8 oz). Store the rest of the cheese for another use.

Preheat the oven to Gas Mark 4/180°C/350°F.

Heat 25 g (1 oz) of the butter with the oil in a frying pan and gently fry the onion until it is soft. Add the tomatoes, chilli powder and salt and pepper and simmer for 5–10 minutes until the mixture is well blended and fairly thick. Add the breadcrumbs, raisins, pickles, olives and the reserved grated cheese. Add the prawns and then fold the eggs gently but thoroughly into the mixture.

Remove the cheese shells from the soaking water and pat dry with kitchen paper. Stuff with the prawn mixture and place one half on top of the other to make a whole cheese. Using the remaining butter, grease a round baking dish 12 cm (5 inches) deep and just large enough to hold the cheese comfortably so that it will not spread and collapse while baking. Put the cheese into the baking dish and bake in the oven, uncovered, for 30 minutes, until the top is bubbly.

Slide the cheese on to a warmed platter, cut into wedges and serve at once. Or serve directly from the baking dish. It will not wait.

## POISSON EN BLAFF

Poached fish                                    Serves 2

Preparation time: 10 minutes + 1 hour marinating + 15 minutes cooking

### For the marinade:

6 tablespoons lime or lemon juice

1 small red chilli, de-seeded and chopped very finely

3 garlic cloves, crushed

2 teaspoons salt

450 ml (¾ pint) water

### For the fish:

2 whole fish weighing 500 g (1 lb) each, heads and tails left on, cleaned, e.g. red snapper or any firm white-fleshed fish

300 ml (½ pint) dry white wine

2 teaspoons lime or lemon juice

250 ml (8 fl oz) water

3 large spring onions, white and green parts, chopped

a good pinch of ground allspice

1 bay leaf

1 whole red chilli

*This way of cooking fish in Martinique is typical of the French islands. The name is something of a mystery, but it has been suggested that when a freshly-caught fish is put into the poaching liquid it makes the sound 'blaff'. In the islands melegueta peppercorns would be used. There is some confusion about these and allspice is an excellent substitute.*

In a shallow dish mix together the lime or lemon juice, chopped chilli, garlic, salt and water. Add the fish and, if necessary, add a little more water to cover. Leave to marinate for 1 hour. Lift out the fish and discard the marinade. Halve the fish crossways.

Pour the wine, lime or lemon juice and water into a heavy frying pan large enough to hold the fish comfortably in a single layer. Add the spring onions, allspice, bay leaf and the whole chilli. Bring to a simmer, add the fish and cook on a low heat just below simmering point for about 10 minutes, until the fish is cooked, turning the fish once.

Divide the fish between two deep oval dishes, so that each dish contains one head and one tail portion. Pour the poaching liquid over the fish. Serve with rice.

# POULTRY

## POLLO EN ESCABECHE

Pickled chicken                                                    Serves 6

Preparation time: 15 minutes + 45 minutes cooking + 4 hours or overnight chilling

*1.5 kg (3½lb) chicken, jointed*

*2 onions, sliced thinly*

*6 whole skinned garlic cloves*

*1 small whole green chilli*

*1 bay leaf*

*½ teaspoon dried oregano*

*300 ml (½ pint) olive oil*

*150 ml (¼ pint) white wine vinegar*

*salt and pepper*

**To garnish:**

*12 lettuce leaves*

*1 avocado, sliced*

*1 tomato, sliced*

*12 green olives*

*This is a wonderful cold summer dish, popular in Latin America as well as in the Spanish-speaking Caribbean. It can be made well ahead of time, always useful for summer cooking.*

Season the chicken pieces with salt and pepper. In a heavy casserole large enough to hold the chicken comfortably, arrange the chicken pieces and top with the onion. Add the garlic cloves. Tie the chilli, bay leaf and oregano in a small piece of muslin and add it to the casserole. Pour in the oil and vinegar, bring to a simmer, cover and cook over a very low heat for 45 minutes, or until the chicken is tender.

Lift the chicken out of the casserole and put it in a large bowl. Discard the herb bag and garlic cloves and pour the cooking liquid over the chicken. Refrigerate for at least 4 hours, or overnight.

Serve the chicken with the jellied sauce and the salad garnish of lettuce, avocado, tomato and green olives.

*Pollo en Escabeche (Pickled chicken)*

# ARROZ CON POLLO

Preparation time: 25–35 minutes + 1 hour marinating + 1 hour cooking

2 garlic cloves, crushed

½ teaspoon dried oregano

1 teaspoon salt

¼ teaspoon pepper

2 tablespoons red wine vinegar

1.5 kg (3½ lb) chicken, jointed

3 tablespoons olive oil

1 onion, chopped finely

1 green pepper, cored, de-seeded and chopped

500 g (1 lb) tomatoes, skinned, de-seeded and chopped

1 bay leaf

2 tablespoons chopped fresh coriander or parsley

125 g (4 oz) ham, chopped

900 ml–1 litre (1½–1¾ pints) chicken stock

500 g (1 lb) long-grain rice

1 tablespoon capers

12 pimiento-stuffed green olives, sliced

### To finish:

4 tablespoons dry sherry

125–175 g (4–6 oz) fresh or frozen peas, cooked

½–1 red pepper, peeled, cored, de-seeded and cut into strips

*This is almost universally popular, not just in the Spanish-speaking islands but in Spain, Mexico and Central and South America. It differs, of course, from the parent Spanish recipe, but surprisingly little from island to island. It would not be possible to write of Caribbean cooking without including it.*

In a small bowl mix together the garlic, oregano, salt, pepper and vinegar and rub the mixture into the chicken pieces. Put the chicken into a bowl and let it stand, at room temperature, for 1 hour. Lift the chicken pieces out of the marinade and pat them dry with kitchen paper. Reserve any marinade.

Heat the oil in a frying pan and fry the chicken until the pieces are golden on both sides. Transfer to a casserole.

In the fat remaining in the pan, gently fry the onion and green pepper until soft. Add them to the casserole with any reserved marinade, the tomatoes, bay leaf, coriander or parsley, ham and 450 ml (¾ pint) of the chicken stock. Cover and simmer for 30 minutes.

Lift out the chicken pieces and vegetable mixture and transfer to a bowl. Measure the liquid and add enough of the remaining chicken stock to make up the quantity to 1 litre (1¾ pints). Pour the rice into the casserole. Add the stock and stir. Add the capers, olives and reserved chicken pieces and vegetable mixture. Cover and cook over a low heat for about 30 minutes, until the rice is tender and all the liquid has been absorbed.

Remove the bay leaf from the casserole. Sprinkle the rice with the sherry and top with the peas and red pepper strips . Serve directly from the casserole.

# ASOPAO DE POLLO

Chicken and rice stew                                    Serves 6–8

Preparation time: 40 minutes + about 1½ hours cooking

½ teaspon dried oregano

1 teaspoon salt

2 large garlic cloves,
crushed

¼ teaspoon pepper

¼ teaspoon lime juice

1.25 kg (3 lb) chicken,
jointed

3 tablespoons corn or
groundnut oil

1 onion, chopped finely

1 green pepper, cored, de-
seeded and chopped finely

50 g (2 oz) ham, chopped
coarsely

500 g (1 lb) tomatoes,
skinned, de-seeded and
chopped

500 g (1 lb) long-grain rice

1.5 litres (2½ pints)
chicken stock

175 g (6 oz) cooked peas

1 tablespoon capers

40 g (1½ oz) pimiento-
stuffed green olives

50 g (2 oz) grated
parmesan cheese

2 red peppers, cored, de-
seeded and cut into strips

*This is a classic of the Puerto Rican kitchen. It
cannot be translated literally as it would not make
much sense – soupy of chicken. In the finished dish
the rice is not dry but soupy.*

In a small bowl mix together the oregano, salt,
garlic, pepper and lime juice. Rub the mixture
into the chicken pieces. Heat the oil in a heavy
casserole and fry the chicken pieces until
lightly golden on both sides. Lift out and place
on a plate. Set aside.

Add the onion and green pepper to the
casserole and gently fry until soft. Add the ham
and tomatoes and cook for a few minutes
longer. Return the chicken to the casserole,
with any juices that may have collected on the
plate, and turn to coat with the tomato
mixture. Cover and cook over a low heat for
about 30 minutes, until the chicken is tender.

Lift out the chicken and transfer to a plate.
When the pieces are cool enough to handle,
remove the skin and bones and cut into 5 cm
(2-inch) pieces. Set aside.

Add the rice and chicken stock to the
casserole. Bring to a simmer, cover and cook
over a low heat for about 20 minutes, until the
rice is tender.

Add the peas, capers, olives, cheese and
chicken to the casserole. Lay the red pepper
strips on top of the rice. Cover and cook just
long enough to heat the chicken through. Serve
from the casserole.

# POLLO CON PIÑA A LA ANTIGUA

Chicken with pineapple (Pictured on front cover)          Serves 6

Preparation time: 35 minutes + about 45 minutes cooking

1.5 kg (3½ lb) chicken, jointed

2 tablespoons olive or corn oil

1 onion, chopped finely

1 garlic clove, chopped

1 green pepper, cored, de-seeded and chopped

250 g (8 oz) tomatoes, skinned and chopped

2 tablespoons seedless raisins

*Poultry or meat cooked with fruit are found in the Spanish-speaking islands and indeed throughout Latin America. They are an inheritance of Middle Eastern dishes that came into the Iberian cuisines during the long centuries when the Moors occupied the Peninsula. This dish is typically colonial as the pineapple is a New World fruit, originating in Brazil.*

Season the chicken pieces with salt and pepper. Heat the oil in a frying pan and fry the chicken pieces until lightly golden. Transfer the chicken to a heavy casserole large enough to

*Asopao de Pollo (Chicken and rice stew)*

2 small chillies, de-seeded and chopped

2 tablespoons chopped fresh coriander

300 ml (½ pint) chicken stock

500 g (1 lb) fresh pineapple, peeled, chopped and juice reserved, or 432 g (15 oz) can of pineapple pieces in natural juice

4 tablespoons white rum

salt and pepper

hold the pieces comfortably.

In the oil remaining in the pan, gently fry the onion, garlic and pepper until tender. Add the tomatoes, raisins, chillies and coriander and simmer for a few minutes to blend the flavours.

Transfer the contents of the frying pan to the casserole with the chicken and pour in enough chicken stock barely to cover. Cover and cook over a low heat for about 45 minutes, until the chicken is tender. Half-way through cooking, add the pineapple and its juice. If the liquid is too abundant, cook partially covered for the remaining cooking time. Pour in the rum 5 minutes before serving. Serve with rice.

*Pollo con Piña a la Antigua (Chicken with pineapple)*

*Almond Chicken*

# ALMOND CHICKEN

Preparation time: 30 minutes + 10 minutes cooking

4 tablespoons groundnut or corn oil

3 skinless boneless chicken breasts, sliced thinly

75 g (3 oz) onion, chopped finely

4 large spring onions, white and green parts, chopped

175 g (6 oz) cucumber, peeled and chopped coarsely

175 g (6 oz) carrots, chopped

125 g (4 oz) mushrooms, sliced

227 g (8 oz) can of water chestnuts, drained and chopped

227 g (8 oz) can of bamboo shoots, drained and chopped

5 cm (2-inch) piece of fresh root ginger, peeled and sliced very thinly

4 tablespoons soy sauce

butter for frying

75 g (3 oz) flaked almonds

*This dish from Trinidad demonstrates perfectly the many racial influences in the Caribbean kitchen. Here Chinese predominates with stir-frying. Everything can be prepared ahead of time and then cooked very quickly.*

Heat the oil in a heavy frying pan or wok and stir-fry the chicken over a brisk heat for 3 minutes. Chop-sticks are ideal for stirring. Add the onion, spring onions, cucumber, carrots, mushrooms, water chestnuts, bamboo shoots and ginger and cook, stirring constantly, over a brisk heat for 3 minutes longer. Pour the soy sauce over the mixture and cook, without stirring, for 1 minute.

Melt a little butter in a small frying pan and fry the flaked almonds for about 1 minute, until they are golden.

Pile the chicken mixture into a heated serving dish, top with the almonds and serve with rice.

# LE CANETON AU RHUM

Preparation time: 25 minutes + 2¾ hours cooking

*2.25–2.75 kg (5–6 lb) duckling*

*900 ml (1½ pints) water*

*40 g (1½ oz) butter*

*1 onion, chopped finely*

*2 garlic cloves, chopped*

*a bouquet garni (a sprig of fresh parsley, ¼ teaspoon each of dried thyme and marjoram and 1 bay leaf, tied in muslin)*

*a good pinch of ground allspice*

*150 ml (¼ pint) dark rum, preferably Guadeloupe rhum*

*salt and pepper*

*The rum of the French islands is very richly flavoured, especially the dark rum used in this recipe from Guadeloupe. It marries particularly well with the rich flavour of duckling. If rum from the French islands is not available, use any good, dark rum.*

Make the stock ahead of time. Remove the giblets from the duckling and place in a saucepan. Pour in the water and simmer, covered, over a moderate heat for 1 hour.

Strain the stock. Reduce over a brisk heat, uncovered, until the stock measures 300 ml (½ pint). Season with salt and pepper and set aside.

Pull any loose fat from the cavity of the duckling and season the bird with salt and pepper. Melt the butter in a large casserole that will hold the duckling comfortably and lightly brown the duckling all over. Lift it out of the casserole and transfer to a platter.

Spoon off all but 2 tablespoons of the fat in the casserole and gently fry the onion and garlic until tender. Return the bird to the casserole with the bouquet garni, allspice and giblet stock. Bring the liquid to a simmer, cover and cook for about 1½ hours, until the duckling is tender.

Discard the bouquet garni and spoon off and discard any fat that has accumulated. Warm the rum, pour it over the duckling and light it. Stand back from the casserole when doing this. When the flames die down, lift out the duck and place on a warm platter. Boil the sauce to reduce it if necessary and pour into a gravy-boat. Serve with rice.

# CHICKEN FRICASSEE

Preparation time: 35 minutes + 3–4 hours or overnight marinating + 45 minutes cooking

4 garlic cloves, crushed

1 teaspoon paprika

2.5 cm (1-inch) piece of fresh root ginger, peeled and grated

¼ teaspoon ground allspice

1.5 kg (3½ lb) chicken, jointed

25 g (1 oz) butter

2 tablespoons groundnut or corn oil

2 onions, chopped finely

1 green pepper, cored, de-seeded and chopped

375 g (12 oz) tomatoes, skinned, de-seeded and chopped

1 whole chilli with stem

350 ml (12 fl oz) chicken stock

salt and pepper

*This is one of Jamaica's most popular dishes. It is deceptive in its simplicity. The medley of flavourings transform the chicken and blend into the sauce. It is good served with rice or with any of the local root vegetables (page 12).*

Mix together the garlic, paprika, ginger, allspice and salt and pepper and rub into the chicken. Put into a container, cover and refrigerate overnight or for 3–4 hours.

When ready to cook, scrape off and reserve the seasonings. Pat the chicken pieces dry with kitchen paper. In a heavy frying pan heat the butter and oil and fry the chicken pieces until golden on both sides. Lift out and transfer to a heavy flameproof casserole.

In the fat remaining in the pan, gently fry the onions and green pepper until tender. Add them to the casserole. Add the tomatoes, reserved seasonings, chilli and chicken stock. Bring to a simmer and cook, covered, over a low heat until the chicken is tender.

Remove and discard the chilli. Lift out the chicken and transfer to a warmed platter. If the sauce is at all watery, reduce it over a brisk heat for a few minutes. Pour the sauce over the chicken and serve.

*Chicken Fricassee*

# POULET AU LAIT DE COCO

Chicken with coconut milk                                    Serves 6

Preparation time: 25 minutes + about 45 minutes cooking

4 tablespoons groundnut oil

1.5 kg (3½ lb) chicken, jointed

2 large onions, chopped finely

1 tablespoon mild curry powder

a few saffron strands, crushed, or a pinch of paprika

2 small red chillies, de-seeded and chopped

450 ml (¾ pint) coconut milk (page 10)

salt and pepper

*This dish from Haiti aptly demonstrates the eclectic character of Caribbean cooking. The French probably introduced the curry from their Indian enclave, Spain contributed the saffron and the chicken, while the New World livened-up the whole dish with chillies.*

Heat the oil in a frying pan and fry the chicken pieces until they are golden on both sides. Transfer them to a casserole large enough to hold them comfortably.

In the oil remaining in the pan, gently fry the onions until they are golden. Add the curry powder, saffron or paprika and chillies. Stir to mix and fry over a moderate heat for about 4 minutes longer.

Scrape the mixture into the casserole. Season with salt and pepper, pour in the coconut milk, cover and cook over a low heat for about 45 minutes, until the chicken is tender. Serve with rice.

# CHICHARRONES DE POLLO

Marinated fried chicken                                    Serves 6

Preparation time: 20 minutes + 3 hours marinating + 40 minutes cooking

4 tablespoons soy sauce

4 tablespoons white rum

4 tablespoons lime or lemon juice

1.75 kg (4 lb) chicken thighs, halved

125 g (4 oz) plain flour

½ teaspoon chilli powder

450 ml (¾ pint) groundnut or corn oil

salt and pepper

1 lemon, sliced, to garnish

*The name of this Dominican dish is a metaphor, since* chicharrones *are pork cracklings and cooks thought the fried chicken, coloured brown by soy sauce, resembled cracklings. This dish has a clear Chinese influence and belongs to the great family of stir-fry dishes.*

In a large bowl combine the soy sauce, rum and lime or lemon juice. Add the chicken pieces and mix well. Leave to marinate at room temperature for 3 hours, turning the pieces from time to time.

Season the flour with the chilli powder and salt and pepper. Remove the chicken from the marinade and pat the pieces dry with kitchen paper. Roll the chicken in the seasoned flour.

Heat the oil in a large, heavy frying pan and fry the chicken pieces, a few at a time, until browned and cooked through – about 6 minutes on each side. Keep the cooked pieces warm while frying the remaining pieces. Serve garnished with the lemon slices and accompanied, if liked, by rice. Serve immediately.

# MEAT

## STOBÁ DI CONCOMBER

Lamb and cucumber stew                                    Serves 6

Preparation time: 20 minutes + 2 hours cooking

*3 tablespoons corn or
groundnut oil*

*1.25 kg (3 lb) lean,
boneless lamb, cut into
5–8 cm (2–3-inch) cubes*

*2 onions, chopped finely*

*2 garlic cloves, chopped*

*2 celery sticks, chopped*

*1 green pepper, cored, de-
seeded and chopped*

*2 small chillies, de-seeded
and chopped*

*250 g (8 oz) tomatoes,
skinned, de-seeded and
chopped*

*2 tablespoons lime or lemon
juice*

*1 tablespoon white wine
vinegar*

*½ teaspoon ground cumin*

*300 ml (½ pint) lamb
stock or water*

*750 g (1½ lb) cucumbers,
chopped coarsely*

*6 small new potatoes*

*salt and pepper*

*The cucumbers used in this stew from Curaçao are
a small, round tropical variety called apple or lemon
cucumbers. The cucumbers available here are an
excellent substitute.*

Heat the oil in a heavy casserole and lightly
brown the lamb pieces all over. Add the
onions, garlic, celery, green pepper, chillies
and tomatoes and cook until soft. Add the lime
or lemon juice, vinegar, cumin, stock or water
and salt and pepper. Bring to a simmer, cover
and cook over a low heat for about 1½ hours,
until the lamb is tender.

Add the cucumbers and potatoes to the
casserole and cook for about 15 minutes longer,
until the potatoes are done.

*Stobá di Concomber (Lamb
and cucumber stew)
Salpicón (Meat salad)*

# SALPICÓN

Preparation time: 40 minutes

### For the salad:

375 g (12 oz) cold roast beef, diced

375 g (12 oz) cold roast chicken, diced

500 g (1 lb) cold boiled potatoes, diced

1 green pepper, cored, de-seeded and chopped

1 red pepper, cored, de-seeded and chopped

375 g (12 oz) fresh pineapple chunks

125 g (4 oz) crisp lettuce, shredded

2 spring onions, white and green parts, chopped

1 tablespoon capers

50 g (2 oz) pimiento-stuffed green olives, halved

### For the vinaigrette:

175 ml (6 fl oz) olive oil

4 tablespoons white wine vinegar

salt and pepper

### To garnish:

watercress sprigs

*This traditional Cuban salad makes a very attractive main course for a summer weekend lunch or dinner. It is hearty enough to satisfy appetites without being heavy. It can be prepared ahead of time and tossed with the dressing at the last minute.*

In a large salad bowl combine the meat, potatoes, peppers, pineapple, lettuce, spring onions, capers and olives.

In a small bowl mix together the oil, vinegar and salt and pepper, whisking to blend.

Pour the dressing over the salad and toss lightly. Garnish with watercress sprigs.

# GRIOTS DE PORC

Preparation time: 20–25 minutes + 2 hours marinating + 1½ hours cooking

*1.25 kg (3 lb) boneless pork loin, cut into 4 cm (1½-inch cubes)*

*1 onion, chopped finely*

*4 spring onions, white and green parts, chopped*

*½ teaspoon dried thyme*

*2 garlic cloves, chopped*

*300 ml (½ pint) Seville (bitter) orange juice, or 100 ml (3½ fl oz) lime or lemon juice mixed with 200 ml (7 fl oz) orange juice*

*1 small chilli, de-seeded and chopped*

*125 ml (4 fl oz) corn, groundnut or vegetable oil*

*salt and pepper*

*Originally Portuguese, but transformed by travel, this dish turns up in islands as diverse as Haiti and Trinidad. The crisp morsels can be served to accompany drinks. When accompanied by rice or a starchy vegetable and a hot chilli sauce, such as Sauce Ti-malice (Hot pepper sauce, page 72), they make an attractive main course. If Seville (bitter) orange juice is not available, a mix of lime juice and orange juice is an acceptable substitute.*

In a heavy casserole combine the pork with the onion, spring onions, thyme, garlic, orange juice, chilli and salt and pepper. Stir to mix and leave to marinate at room temperature for 2 hours.

When ready to cook, pour in enough water to barely cover the pork. Bring to a simmer and cook, covered, over a low heat for about 1 hour, or until the pork is tender. Drain and discard the liquid. Set aside the meat and vegetable mixture.

Rinse out and dry the casserole. Pour in and heat the oil. Add the meat and vegetable mixture to the casserole and fry until the pork pieces are brown and crispy. Lift out with a slotted spoon to a warm platter and serve.

*Variation*: Reserve the cooking liquid, boil until reduced and serve as a sauce with the pork.

# PICADILLO

Preparation time: 25 minutes + about 30 minutes cooking

*4 tablespoons olive oil*

*2 onions, chopped finely*

*1 large green pepper, cored, de-seeded and chopped*

*2 garlic cloves, chopped*

*1 small chilli, de-seeded and chopped*

*1 kg (2 lb) lean minced beef*

*500 g (1 lb) tomatoes, skinned, de-seeded and chopped*

*½ teaspoon ground cumin*

*50 g (2 oz) seedless raisins*

*50 g (2 oz) pimiento-stuffed green olives, halved*

*1 tablespoon capers*

*salt and pepper*

*Undoubtedly one of Cuba's most popular dishes, picadillo can be made special with the addition of side dishes like Fried Ripe Plantains (page 70), black beans and rice, with each portion topped with a fried egg. The dish is also a favourite in parts of Latin America. It can be served more simply just accompanied by rice. In Cuba achiote (annatto) oil is used; olive oil is a good substitute.*

Heat the oil in a frying pan large enough to hold all the ingredients. Gently fry the onions, green pepper, garlic and chilli until soft. Add the beef and cook, stirring with a wooden spoon to break up the meat, until brown all over. Add the tomatoes, cumin and salt and pepper to taste and stir to mix. Add the raisins and simmer, uncovered, over a moderate heat for about 25 minutes, or until the meat is cooked and the mixture well blended.

Add the olives and capers to the mince and cook for 5 minutes longer before serving.

# CURRIED LAMB

Preparation time: 45 minutes + about 2 hours cooking

*2–3 tablespoons corn or groundnut oil*

*1.25 kg (3 lb) lean, boneless lamb, cut into 5 cm (2-inch) pieces*

*2 large onions, chopped finely*

*3 tablespoons mild or hot curry powder, to taste*

*1 bay leaf*

*Curried kid (baby goat) is popular, not just in Jamaica, where this dish originates, but in many islands, especially the English-speaking ones. Montserrat calls its version Goat Water, very off-putting. However the islands also make excellent curried lamb, which is much more accessible.*

Heat the oil in a frying pan and brown the lamb pieces lightly all over – in two batches if

*Picadillo (Beef hash)*

¼ teaspoon ground allspice

300 ml (½ pint) coconut milk (page 10)

about 300 ml (½ pint) lamb or chicken stock

2 tablespoons lime or lemon juice

salt and pepper

necessary. Lift out with a slotted spoon and transfer to a heavy casserole.

In the oil remaining in the pan, gently fry the onions until lightly browned. Add the curry powder and fry gently for 2–3 minutes, stirring. Scrape the contents of the pan into the casserole and add the bay leaf, allspice, coconut milk and enough stock to barely cover the meat. Season with salt and pepper, bring to a simmer, cover and cook over a low heat for about 2 hours, until the lamb is tender.

Just before serving, add the lime or lemon juice and cook for a few minutes longer to blend the flavours. Serve with rice.

# RABBIT IN PEANUT SAUCE

Serves 4–6

Preparation time: 15 minutes + about 1¼ hours cooking

1.25 kg (3 lb) rabbit portions

4 tablespoons corn or groundnut oil

1 onion, chopped finely

1 garlic clove, chopped

450 ml (¾ pint) chicken stock or water

1 bay leaf

¼ teaspoon dried thyme

¼ teaspoon dried marjoram

1 tablespoon chopped fresh parsley

¼ teaspoon grated nutmeg

2 chillies, de-seeded and chopped finely

50 g (2 oz) roasted peanuts, ground

salt and pepper

*This way of cooking rabbit is popular throughout the Leeward Islands. It has an unusual but not overly exotic flavour, which explains its popularity in the islands. Rabbit has the virtue of being a very lean meat.*

Season the rabbit pieces with salt and pepper. Heat the oil in a heavy casserole and fry the rabbit until lightly browned on both sides. Add the onion and garlic and gently fry until soft. Add the stock or water, bay leaf, thyme, marjoram, parsley, nutmeg and chillies. Cover and simmer over a low heat for about 1 hour or more, until the rabbit is almost tender.

Add the peanuts to the casserole, stir to mix and simmer for 15 minutes longer, or until the rabbit is tender and the sauce well blended. Serve with rice or any root vegetable (page 12) and one of the hot sauces on pages 72–4.

# DAUBE DE PORC AUX BÉLANGÈRES

Pork stew with aubergines                                    Serves 6

Preparation time: 10 minutes + 2½ hours cooking

*1.25 kg (3 lb) boneless
pork loin in one piece*

*3 tablespoons plain flour*

*3 tablespoons groundnut oil*

*½ teaspoon dried thyme*

*¼ teaspoon dried sage*

*1 small chilli, de-seeded and
chopped*

*¼ teaspoon ground allspice*

*1.25 kg (3 lb) aubergines,
peeled and cut into 2.5 cm
(1-inch) cubes*

*salt and pepper*

*Aubergine is known by a number of different
names in the islands. Though they are of slightly
different varieties, the flavour is much the same.
Pork and aubergine seem natural partners in this
stew from Martinique.*

Coat the pork with the flour, shaking to
remove any excess. Heat the oil in a large
heavy casserole and brown the pork all over.

Add all the remaining ingredients to the
pork, except the aubergine cubes. Add enough
water barely to cover, bring to a simmer, cover
and cook over a low heat for about 2 hours,
until the pork is almost tender.

Add the aubergine cubes to the casserole and
cook for about 30 minutes longer, until the
aubergine and pork are both tender.

Check the seasoning, slice the pork and
serve the stew with rice.

# BIFTECK À LA CRÉOLE

Preparation time: 5–10 minutes + 4 hours marinating + about 10 minutes cooking

2 tablespoons olive oil

2 tablespoons red wine vinegar

2 garlic cloves, crushed

1.25 kg (3 lb) rump steak in one piece about 2.5 cm (1 inch) thick

6 tablespoons dark rum, preferably Martinique or Guadeloupe rhum vieux

salt and pepper

*This is a delicious use of rum and turns a rump steak into a party dish. The French culinary influence in the French-speaking islands of Martinique and Guadeloupe is evident here, though local cooks have added their own special island touch.*

In a large bowl combine the oil, vinegar, garlic and salt and pepper to taste. Add the steak and marinate for about 4 hours, turning it from time to time. Lift the steak out of the marinade and pat it dry with kitchen paper. Reserve the marinade.

Grill the steak to the preferred degree of doneness – about 4 minutes on each side for rare steak. Baste the steak with the reserved marinade during cooking, using it all.

Transfer the steak to a warmed platter and pour over any juices that may have collected in the grill pan. Warm the rum, pour it over the steak and light it. Stand well back when doing this. As soon as the flames die down, carve and serve the steak.

# VEGETABLES AND SALADS

## GLAZED SWEET POTATOES

Serves 4–6

Preparation time: 5 minutes + 45 minutes cooking

1 kg (2 lb) sweet potatoes, peeled and cut into 1 cm (½-inch) slices

40 g (1½ oz) butter, melted, plus extra for greasing

2 tablespoons white rum

25 g (1 oz) light brown soft sugar

salt and pepper

*This root vegetable, which originated in what is now modern Peru, is versatile enough to use in soups and sweets. It is also a welcome addition to a main course instead of its compatriot, the potato, which was first cultivated in the highlands of Peru thousands of years ago. Both vegetables have migrated to the rest of the world. The sweet potato was an early immigrant to the West Indies brought by the Arawaks; it has proved enduringly popular throughout the islands ever since.*

Preheat the oven to Gas Mark 4/180°C/ 350°F.

Cook the sweet potatoes in a saucepan of briskly boiling water for 15–20 minutes, or until tender. Drain.

Grease a baking dish generously with butter and arrange the sweet potato slices in it in an overlapping pattern. Drizzle with the melted butter and rum and sprinkle over the sugar and salt and pepper.

Cover the dish with foil and bake in the oven for 20 minutes. Remove the foil and bake for 10 minutes longer to brown the potatoes lightly. Serve with meat or poultry.

## COO-COO

Serves 6–8

Preparation time: 5 minutes + about 20 minutes cooking

1.5 litres (2½ pints) chicken stock or water

*This dish is generally credited to Barbados, though it turns up in a great many islands in various forms and with differing ingredients. The name* coo-coo

*12 small okra, trimmed and cut into 5 mm (¼-inch) slices*

*½ teaspoon salt, if necessary*

*250 g (8 oz) yellow maize meal*

*40 g (1½ oz) butter*

means a cooked side dish, and in Barbados this version would be served with the island speciality, fried flying fish. It is an interesting one as it contains okra, brought to the New World by African slaves. Cold coo-coo can be sliced and fried in butter or oil. It is a good accompaniment to any plainly-cooked meat, poultry or fish. It is not unlike Italian polenta, though it is, of course, the earlier dish.

Bring the stock or water to a boil in a large saucepan. Add the okra slices and, if using water instead of stock, the salt. Bring to a simmer and cook, covered, for 10 minutes.

Pour in the maize meal in a slow, steady stream, stirring constantly with a wooden spoon. Cook over a moderate heat, stirring, for about 5 minutes, or until thick and smooth.

Turn the mixture into a buttered large shallow bowl and leave to mould for a few minutes. Turn out onto a warmed platter and spread with the rest of the butter.

# FRIED SWEET POTATOES

Serves 4–6

Preparation time: 5 minutes + 15 minutes soaking + about 15 minutes cooking

*1 kg (2 lb) sweet potatoes, peeled and cut into 1 cm (½-inch) slices*

*corn or groundnut oil for deep-frying*

*salt and pepper*

This is a simple and attractive way of cooking sweet potatoes that is popular island-wide. It makes a change from the more usual baked potatoes, good though these certainly are.

Put the sweet potato slices into cold salted water and leave to soak for 15 minutes. Drain and pat dry with kitchen paper.

Heat enough oil for deep-frying to 190°C/375°F on a frying thermometer. Deep-fry the sweet potato slices for about 15 minutes, or until tender and brown. Lift out and drain on kitchen paper. Season with salt and pepper. Serve with meat or poultry.

# ENSALADA DE MOLONDRONES Y TOMATES

Okra and tomato salad                              Serves 6–8

Preparation and cooking time: 40 minutes

500 g (1 lb) small okra, trimmed

2 tablespoons lime or lemon juice

2 teaspoons salt

250 g (8 oz) tomatoes, skinned, de-seeded and chopped coarsely

**For the dressing:**

3 tablespoons olive, corn, groundnut or vegetable oil

1 tablespoon red or white wine vinegar

salt and pepper

**To serve:**

lettuce leaves

Okra are of tropical Asian origin but were introduced into the islands by Africans. They are known by a number of names – in the Dominican Republic, where this salad originates, as molondrones or quimbombós. This is an unusual and attractive summer salad.

In a bowl mix the okra with the lime or lemon juice and enough cold water barely to cover. Leave to stand for 5 minutes. Drain thoroughly.

Cook the okra in boiling water with the salt for about 10 minutes until tender. Drain and cool.

To make the dressing, beat together the oil, vinegar and salt and pepper in a small bowl.

In a bowl combine the okra with the tomatoes. Pour the dressing over the vegetables and toss lightly to mix. Serve on salad plates lined with lettuce leaves.

# CONCOMBRES EN SALADE

Cucumber salad                                     Serves 4

Preparation time: 25 minutes

1 cucumber, peeled, halved lengthways, de-seeded and chopped

1 teaspoon salt

1 garlic clove, crushed

1 tablespoon lime or lemon juice

1 small red chilli, de-seeded and chopped

lettuce leaves, to serve

This refreshing, unusual and yet very simple salad is typical of the cooking of the French islands.

Mix the cucumber with the salt and let it stand for 10 minutes. Drain thoroughly.

In a bowl combine the cucumber with the garlic, lime or lemon juice and chilli. Toss to mix and serve on salad plates lined with lettuce leaves.

*Avocado and Tomato Salad*

# AVOCADO AND TOMATO SALAD

Serves 4

Preparation time: 15–20 minutes

*500 g (1lb) tomatoes, skinned, de-seeded and chopped*

*2 avocados, peeled, stoned and sliced crossways*

**For the dressing:**

*3 tablespoons corn or groundnut oil*

*1 tablespoon lime or lemon juice*

*½ small red chilli, de-seeded and chopped finely*

*salt and pepper*

**To serve:**

*lettuce leaves*

*Many dishes turn up in a number of islands and it is often hard to identify their island of origin, since cooks island-hop even more than tourists do. However, they all have an unmistakable Caribbean touch.*

Put the tomatoes in a bowl.

To make the dressing, in a small bowl beat together the oil, lime or lemon juice, chilli and salt and pepper. Pour over the tomatoes.

Add the avocado slices to the salad – these are best left until last as they discolour easily – and fold gently into the tomatoes. Serve on salad plates lined with lettuce leaves.

*Ensalada de Molondrones y Tomates (Okra and tomato salad)*

*Concombres en Salade (Cucumber salad)*

# MOROS Y CRISTIANOS

Moors and Christians                                    Serves 4–6

Preparation time: 15 minutes + about 2½ hours cooking

**For the beans:**

175 g (6 oz) black beans

350 ml (12 fl oz) cold water

½ teaspoon salt

**For the beans and rice:**

2 tablespoons olive oil

1 onion, chopped finely

1 garlic clove, chopped

1 green pepper, cored, de-seeded and chopped coarsely

250 g (8 oz) tomatoes, skinned, de-seeded and chopped

½ teaspoon sugar

250 g (8 oz) long-grain rice

450 ml (¾ pint) water

salt and pepper

*This is a very old colonial dish going back to the early days of Spanish occupation of the island of Cuba. Black haricot beans had arrived from their original home in Mexico and the Spanish brought in rice. Local cooks put the two together, and since Spain had only just reconquered its own country from the centuries-long Moorish occupation, and memories of the struggle were still fresh, the name must have seemed apt. It is interesting that this dish has returned to Spain, where it is an accepted part of Spanish cuisine. Unsurprisingly it can be met with in South American cooking – simple proof of how good the combination is. Leftover black beans may be used for the dish.*

Wash the beans thoroughly but do not soak them. Put them into a large saucepan with the cold water and salt, bring to the boil and boil for 10 minutes. Cover and simmer over a low heat for about 2 hours, or until they are tender: the time will depend on how fresh the beans are. If the beans seem to be drying out, add a little hot water from time to time. The beans should be tender but firm, as they will cook a little longer with the rice. Drain and set aside.

Heat the oil in a heavy saucepan or a casserole with a lid and add the onion, garlic and pepper. Fry gently over a moderate heat for about 5 minutes, until they are tender but not brown. Add the tomatoes and cook for about 5 minutes until the mixture is thick and well blended. Season to taste with the sugar and salt and pepper.

Fold the beans into the tomatoes, mixing gently but thoroughly. Stir in the rice and water, mixing lightly. Cover and cook over a very low heat for about 20 minutes, until the rice is tender and all the water has been absorbed.

Serve the beans and rice to accompany a meat dish, or serve with Fried Ripe Plantains (page 70).

*Variation*: Cook the rice and beans separately, allowing the beans a little longer cooking time to become quite tender. Serve the rice in a ring with the beans in the centre.

## BEREHEIN NA FORNO

Aubergine in coconut milk                                    Serves 4–6

Preparation time: 15 minutes + 55 minutes cooking

*15 g (½ oz) butter, softened, for greasing*

*500 g (1 lb) aubergines, peeled and sliced thinly*

*3 onions, chopped finely*

*1 red chilli, de-seeded and chopped*

*200 g (7 oz) creamed coconut*

*350 ml (12 fl oz) hot water*

*salt and pepper*

*The Netherlands and France share the tiny island known as both St Maarten and St Martin. Both maintain quite distinctive cuisines within a Caribbean framework: this particular dish is from the former. Coconut milk is used a great deal in island cooking; though it is easy enough to make from a fresh coconut (page 10), it is very much easier and just as satisfactory to make it using creamed coconut, which simply needs diluting to the desired consistency.*

Preheat the oven to Gas Mark 4/180°C/350°F.

Butter an ovenproof dish large enough to hold the aubergine slices comfortably in an overlapping layer. Cover the aubergines with a layer of onion, sprinkle with the chilli and season to taste with salt and pepper.

Dissolve the creamed coconut in the hot water and pour over the aubergines. Cover the dish with a lid or foil and bake in the oven for 45 minutes. Uncover and bake for 10 minutes longer.

# LA SALADE DE BANANE VERTE

Green banana salad                                    Serves 6

Preparation and cooking time: 35 minutes

*4 semi-green bananas, peeled*

*1 teaspoon salt*

*250 g (8 oz) tomatoes, skinned, de-seeded and chopped*

*½ cucumber, peeled and chopped*

*2 celery sticks, chopped*

*1 avocado, peeled, stoned and sliced crossways*

**For the dressing:**

*125 ml (4 fl oz) olive or vegetable oil*

*2 tablespoons white wine vinegar*

*2 teaspoons Dijon mustard*

*1 garlic clove, crushed*

*salt and pepper*

**To serve:**

*lettuce leaves*

*This Martinique salad uses a mixture of Caribbean and French ingredients: cooked semi-green bananas and a traditional vinaigrette dressing meet in the salad bowl. The result of this culinary mix is good indeed.*

Put the bananas into a saucepan with the salt and water to cover. Bring to a simmer and cook, covered, for 10–15 minutes, until they are tender. Drain, cool and cut into 1 cm (½-inch) slices.

To make the dressing, combine the oil, vinegar, mustard, garlic and salt and pepper in a bowl. Beat with a fork to mix.

Combine the bananas, tomatoes, cucumber, celery and avocado with the vinaigrette dressing in a bowl. Toss lightly to mix. Serve on salad plates lined with lettuce leaves.

# RICE AND PEAS

                                                    Serves 6–8

Preparation time: overnight soaking + 10 minutes + 1½–2 hours cooking

*175 g (6 oz) red kidney beans*

*Rice and Peas*
*La Salade de Banane Verte*
*(Green banana salad)*

*English-speaking islanders use the terms peas and beans interchangably, so that in Jamaica red kidney beans are called peas. This famous Jamaican dish is sometimes made with fresh pigeon (gunga) peas when they are in season. Coconut milk gives the dish a very subtle flavour.*

| 2 tablespoons corn, groundnut or vegetable oil |
| --- |
| 1 onion, chopped finely |
| 1 small red chilli, de-seeded and chopped |
| 100 g (3½ oz) creamed coconut |
| 400 ml (14 fl oz) hot water |
| ½ teaspoon dried thyme |
| 500 g (1 lb) long-grain rice |
| salt and pepper |

Put the beans into a large, heavy saucepan with cold water to cover and leave to soak overnight.

When ready to cook, drain and discard the soaking water. Rinse the beans and return to the pan with cold water to cover by about 5 cm (2 inches). Bring to the boil and boil rapidly for 10 minutes. Reduce the heat to a simmer and cook, covered, over a moderate heat for 1–1½ hours, or until the beans are almost tender: they will cook for about 30 minutes longer with the rice.

Drain the beans and measure the liquid. Make up the liquid to 450 ml (¾ pint) with cold water if necessary. Return the beans and liquid to the saucepan.

Heat the oil in a frying pan and gently fry the onion until it is golden. Add it to the saucepan with the chilli.

Dissolve the creamed coconut in the hot water. Add it to the saucepan with the thyme, rice and salt and pepper to taste. Stir gently to mix, cover and cook over a very low heat for about 30 minutes, or until the rice and beans are tender and all the liquid has been absorbed.

## FRIED RIPE PLANTAINS

(Pictured on page 5)                                      Serves 4–6

Preparation time: 5 minutes + about 10 minutes cooking

| 3 ripe plantains |
| --- |
| 50 g (2 oz) butter |
| salt |

*The skins of ripe plantains are quite black but the plantains must still be cooked before they can be eaten. They are a standard side dish in Cuba and other Spanish islands, where they are called Plátanos Fritos Maduros. In the French-speaking islands they are known as Bananes Frites and are often served as a dessert, when they are sprinkled with sugar and flamed with rum after they have been fried. In most islands they accompany meat dishes, such as Picadillo (Beef hash, page 56).*

Cut off both ends of the plantains, peel and halve lengthways. Slice the halved plantains in half crossways, giving 12 slices in all.

Heat the butter in a frying pan and fry the plantain slices over a moderate heat until browned on both sides – about 4 minutes a side. Drain on kitchen paper, sprinkle with salt and serve immediately.

# ALU TALKARI

| Potato curry | Serves 4 |
|---|---|

Preparation time: 10 minutes + 25 minutes cooking

4 tablespoons corn, groundnut or vegetable oil

1 tablespoon fenugreek seeds (optional)

2 garlic cloves, chopped

2 tablespoons mild or hot curry powder, to taste

1 kg (2 lb) potatoes, peeled and cut into 1 cm (½-inch) cubes

250 ml (8 fl oz) water

salt

*Like most dishes in the Caribbean, this Trinidad dish has evolved from the original recipe – in this case an Indian one, as there are many people of Indian origin in Trinidad. It makes a perfect lunch or supper dish when stuffed into Roti, an Indian bread (page 83).*

Heat the oil in a frying pan that has a lid and add the fenugreek seeds, if using, and the garlic. Fry gently over a moderate heat until the garlic is browned. Lift out the garlic and fenugreek, if using, with a slotted spoon and discard.

Add the curry powder to the frying pan and cook, stirring with a wooden spoon, for 3–4 minutes. Add the potatoes, water and salt. Cover and simmer for about 20 minutes, until the potatoes are tender. If the potatoes seem to be drying out during cooking, add a little hot water, although the finished dish should be quite dry. Serve as a side dish or use to stuff Roti.

# SAUCES

## PEPPER WINE

Makes 450 ml (¾ pint)

Preparation time: 5 minutes + 10 days standing

*8 small whole red or green chillies with stems*

*450 ml (¾ pint) white rum, dry sherry or cider or light malt vinegar*

*This is an extremely useful flavoured rum, sherry or vinegar from Jamaica. Just a few drops lift a dish out of the ordinary and add a special zest.*

Pack the chillies into a glass jar and pour in the liquid. Cover tightly and store in a cool, dark place or in the refrigerator. Allow to stand for 10 days before using.

Add a few drops to soups, stews or sauces. It keeps indefinitely.

## SAUCE TI-MALICE

Hot pepper sauce

Makes 300 ml (½ pint)

Preparation time: 10–15 minutes + 1 hour marinating + 5 minutes cooking

*125 g (4 oz) onions, chopped finely*

*4 spring onions, white and green parts, chopped*

*125 ml (4 fl oz) lime or lemon juice*

*2 garlic cloves, chopped finely*

*1 tablespoon finely chopped red or yellow chillies*

*4 tablespoons olive oil*

*salt and pepper*

*This is another of the chilli sauces, this time from Haiti. Its name suggests its prankish nature, the heat of the sauce not appearing at first taste. It is good with almost any meat or poultry, particularly Griots de Porc (Glazed pork pieces, page 55).*

In a small bowl combine the onions, spring onions and lime or lemon juice and leave to marinate for 1 hour.

Transfer the marinade to a saucepan and add the remaining ingredients. Bring to a simmer and cook over a moderate heat for 2 minutes. Transfer to a bowl and cool. Serve cold.

*Pepper Wine
Sauce Ti-malice (Hot
pepper sauce)*

# HOT PEPPER RELISH

(Pictured on page 5)     Makes about 125 g (4 oz)

Preparation time: 30 minutes + 15–30 minutes cooking

*125 g (4 oz) red chillies, de-seeded and chopped*

*125 g (4 oz) onions, chopped finely*

*salt*

*Caribbean sauces and relishes are legion, especially those made with fresh, very hot chillies. Recipes vary from island to island, but all use hot chillies. This particular one is popular in St Kitts. One of the favourite chillies used is the* Habañero, *known in Jamaica as the Scotch Bonnet.*

In a small, heavy saucepan combine the chillies and onions and cook, uncovered, over a very low heat for 15–30 minutes, stirring from time to time, until the mixture is thick. It may be necessary to add a little water during cooking if the mixture looks too dry. Season with salt and cool.

Use sparingly as a sauce with any plainly-cooked fish, poultry or meat.

# PAW-PAW SAUCE

Preparation time: 10 minutes + 1 hour cooking

*1 kg (2 lb) paw-paw, peeled, de-seeded and cubed*

*600 ml (1 pint) water*

*3 cloves*

*2 tablespoons sugar*

*125 ml (4 fl oz) lime or lemon juice*

*This Jamaican sauce is sometimes called paw-paw apple sauce in the islands: the climate is not good for apple growing and this makes an acceptable, indeed delicious, substitute. Paw-paw is named from the Paw-paw Indians of Jamaica, though it is known as papaya in the Spanish-speaking islands and in most of North and South America. First cultivated in Mexico, it is now grown in most of the tropical countries of the world.*

Combine all the ingredients in a heavy saucepan large enough to hold them comfortably. Bring to a simmer over a moderate heat, cover and cook for about 1 hour, or until the paw-paw is tender and most of the liquid has been absorbed. Remove the lid for the last 15 minutes of cooking to evaporate excess liquid if necessary.

Remove the pan from the heat and discard the cloves. Purée the mixture in a food processor or push it through a sieve: it should have the consistency of apple sauce. Serve hot or cold, with pork or any meat or poultry, or whenever apple sauce would be used.

# BREADS, PUDDINGS AND DESSERTS

## RUM SAUCE

Makes 350 ml (12 fl oz)

Preparation time: 10 minutes + 5 minutes cooking

*1½ tablespoons cornflour*

*2 tablespoons cold water*

*3 tablespoons sugar, or more to taste*

*250 ml (8 fl oz) orange juice*

*125 ml (4 fl oz) white or dark rum*

*This sauce is popular in all the English-speaking islands. Traditionally it is served with Carrot Pudding (page 79). It is also very good with Christmas pudding and is delicious poured hot over Ice Cream (page 86).*

In a small saucepan mix together the cornflour, cold water and sugar. Stir in the orange juice and cook, stirring from time to time, over a moderate heat for about 5 minutes, until the mixture is lightly thickened.

Leave to cool and then stir in the rum. Serve warm or hot.

# FLOATING ISLANDS

(Pictured on page 4) Serves 6

Preparation time: 15 minutes + 25 minutes cooking

### For the custard:

3 large egg yolks (size 1 or 2)

50 g (2 oz) caster sugar

450 ml (¾ pint) single cream

1 teaspoon vanilla essence

### For the islands:

2 tablespoons guava preserve

1 large egg white (size 1 or 2)

### To finish:

125 ml (4 fl oz) double cream

1 tablespoon caster sugar

2–4 tablespoons white rum, preferably Jamaican

This is a very old dish in the islands. Both Jamaica and Barbados claim it for their own, and it turns up in many other islands as well as these two. Clearly, once upon a time, it evolved from the French dessert Oeufs à la Neige (Snow eggs). The main difference is that in the French and presumably original recipe, the egg whites are formed into egg shapes and poached. In the island version they are uncooked.

Combine the egg yolks and sugar in the top of a double boiler off the heat. Whisk until the egg yolks are light and lemon-coloured and well mixed with the sugar.

In a small saucepan heat the single cream to scalding point. Pour it into the egg mixture in a thin, steady stream, whisking constantly. Add hot water to the bottom of the double boiler and cook the custard over a very low heat, stirring constantly with a wooden spoon, until the mixture is thick enough to coat the spoon. Do not let it boil. Cover to prevent a skin forming and leave to cool.

Stir the vanilla essence into the custard, pour into a glass serving dish and refrigerate.

Beat the guava preserve lightly with a fork and set aside. In a large bowl beat the egg white until it stands in firm peaks. Add the preserve to the egg white, continuing to beat until thoroughly incorporated.

Whip the double cream with the sugar until stiff. Stir in the rum and whip for a few minutes longer until stiff again.

Remove the custard from the refrigerator. Drop the beaten egg white mixture by tablespoon onto the custard to form the islands. Spoon the rum cream around the outer edge of the serving dish, or serve separately. Serve the pudding the same day it is made.

# BANANA BREAD

Makes a 1 kg (2 lb) loaf

Preparation time: 20 minutes + about 1 hour cooking

*250 g (8 oz) plain flour*

*1 teaspoon baking powder*

*2 teaspoons cream of tartar*

*½ teaspoon salt*

*½ teaspoon grated nutmeg*

*125g (4 oz) unsalted butter, softened, plus extra for greasing*

*125 g (4 oz) sugar*

*2 eggs, beaten well*

*500 g (1 lb) very ripe bananas, peeled and mashed*

*Jamaican cooks are noted for the excellence of their teabreads. The breads, which take little time to make, are delicious plain or buttered for tea, or as an accompaniment to a dessert such as Ice Cream (page 86). Banana bread is a particular favourite.*

Preheat the oven to Gas Mark 4/180°C/350°F. Butter a 23 × 13 cm (9- × 5-inch) or 1 kg (2 lb) loaf tin.

Sift the flour, baking powder, cream of tartar, salt and nutmeg into a large bowl.

In another bowl cream the butter and sugar until the mixture is light and fluffy. Beat in the eggs.

Add the sifted ingredients and the mashed banana alternately to the creamed mixture, beating well after each addition. Pour the batter into the loaf tin. Bake in the oven for about 1 hour, or until a skewer comes out clean and the banana bread has shrunk away from the sides of the tin.

Let the bread cool in the tin for about 5 minutes before turning it out onto a wire rack to cool completely.

# CARROT PUDDING

Preparation time: 30 minutes soaking + 15 minutes + 40–50 minutes cooking

*175 g (6 oz) seedless raisins*

*125 ml (4 fl oz) dark rum*

*125 g (4 oz) unsalted butter, plus extra for greasing*

*125 g (4 oz) sugar*

*250 g (8 oz) carrots, grated finely*

*125 g (4 oz) plain flour*

*½ teaspoon salt*

*2 teaspoons baking powder*

*1 teaspoon ground allspice*

*2 large eggs (size 1 or 2), beaten well*

*Carrot pudding has been an English favourite for hundreds of years, which explains why it turns up in so many islands in slightly different versions. This one uses island rum to excellent advantage.*

Put the raisins into a small bowl, pour in the rum and leave to soak for 30 minutes.

Preheat the oven to Gas Mark 4/180°C/ 350°F. Butter a 1-litre (1¾-pint) soufflé dish.

In a large bowl cream the butter with the sugar until light and fluffy. Add the carrots and the soaked raisins and rum, mixing well.

Sift the flour with the salt, baking powder and allspice. Add to the carrot mixture, blend in and then fold in the eggs.

Pour the batter into the soufflé dish. Bake in the oven for 40–50 minutes, or until a skewer comes out clean. Serve warm with hot Rum Sauce (page 76). Or, if preferred, both the pudding and the sauce can be lightly chilled.

# BAKED BANANAS FLAMBÉE

Serves 4

Preparation time: 10 minutes + 15 minutes cooking

125 g (4 oz) unsalted butter

4 large, ripe bananas, peeled and halved lengthways

250 g (8 oz) light brown soft sugar

125 ml (4 fl oz) lime or lemon juice

250 ml (8 fl oz) white rum

2 teaspoons ground allspice

*Island cooks are ingenious in their use of fresh fruits, especially their banana desserts in which they all excel, playing variations on a theme. This very simple dish from Antigua makes a delicious finish to a meal.*

*Baked Bananas Flambée*

*Carrot Pudding with Rum Sauce*

*Coco Quemado (Coconut pudding) with Arrowroot Custard*

Preheat the oven to Gas Mark 6/200°C/400°F.

Generously butter a shallow ovenproof serving dish large enough to hold the bananas in a single layer. Arrange the bananas in the dish, cut-side up. Sprinkle with the sugar.

Mix together the lime or lemon juice, half the rum and the allspice. Sprinkle over the bananas and dot with the rest of the butter.

Bake the bananas in the oven for 15 minutes. Baste half-way through cooking.

Remove the bananas from the oven, warm the remaining rum, pour it over the bananas and set it alight. Serve as soon as the flames die down.

# COCO QUEMADO

Coconut pudding                                                    Serves 6

Preparation time: 10–20 minutes + 20–25 minutes cooking

*500 g (1 lb) sugar*

*250 ml (8 fl oz) water*

*500 g (1 lb) grated coconut (pages 10–11) (about 2 coconuts)*

*4 large egg yolks (size 1 or 2)*

*½ teaspoon ground cinnamon*

*125 ml (4 fl oz) white rum*

*butter for greasing*

Quemado *means, literally, burnt, but here just refers to the light browning, under the grill, of the finished pudding. It is well worth taking the trouble to grate a fresh coconut for the additional flavour and improved texture it gives to this Cuban dish.*

Combine the sugar and water in a saucepan large enough to hold all the ingredients and bring to a simmer. Heat to about 120°C/250°F or until a little of the syrup forms threads when cooled in cold water and tested between the fingers.

Add the grated coconut to the syrup and stir to mix. Stir in the egg yolks, cinnamon and rum and continue to cook, over a low heat, stirring constantly with a wooden spoon, until the mixture is very thick.

Pour the mixture into a buttered shallow flameproof serving dish and place under a hot grill just long enough to lightly brown the top. Serve with whipped cream or Arrowroot Custard (below).

# ARROWROOT CUSTARD

Serves 4–6                                      Makes 600 ml (1 pint)

Preparation time: 10 minutes + about 10 minutes cooking

*2 tablespoons arrowroot*

*410 g (13 oz) can of evaporated milk*

*50 g (2 oz) caster sugar*

*½ teaspoon vanilla essence*

*3 large eggs (size 1 or 2), beaten well*

*The island of St Vincent makes good use of its arrowroot. Here arrowroot makes a delicious light custard to accompany fresh or stewed fruits, or any dessert, for those avoiding cream.*

Mix the arrowroot with a little of the milk in a saucepan. Mix in the rest of the milk and the sugar, bring to a simmer and cook, stirring with a wooden spoon, over a moderate heat for about 1 minute, until thickened.

Add the vanilla essence and eggs to the sauce and continue to cook for just 4–5 minutes, until the mixture forms a smooth custard that coats the spoon. Do not overcook.

Serve with any stewed fruit, or fresh fruit like sliced mangoes or fruit salad. Or serve with any dessert in place of cream.

# ROTI

Serves 4

Preparation time: 15 minutes + 15–20 minutes rising + 20 minutes cooking

*250 g (8 oz) plain flour, plus extra for kneading*

*¼ teaspoon baking powder*

*½ teaspoon salt*

*milk or water to mix*

*ghee (clarified butter) or vegetable oil for brushing*

Roti *simply means bread and this is the term most often used in Trinidad for* parathas, *which is what these are. They are among the classic breads of the Indian sub-continent, brought to the West Indies by immigrant workers. Like everything else in the Caribbean, they have evolved from the original. Roti are served as a bread with curries or, if made a little larger, may be stuffed with a chicken, lamb, prawn or potato curry. The curry is put into the centre of the bread circle which is then folded over like an envelope. Eaten by hand it makes a magnificent lunch.*

Sift the flour, baking powder and salt into a large bowl. Add enough milk or water to make a stiff dough. Alternatively, mix the ingredients in a food processor. Form the dough into a ball and turn it out onto a lightly floured board. Knead the dough thoroughly for about 10 minutes, until it is smooth and pliable.

Form the dough into four equal-sized balls and roll out into 20 cm (8-inch) circles. Brush the dough circles all over with ghee or vegetable oil and again form into balls. Cover with a clean cloth and leave in a warm place for 15–20 minutes.

Roll the balls out again into 20–30 cm (8–12-inch) circles. The larger circles are better for stuffing, the smaller ones better as an accompanying bread.

Heat a heavy frying pan or griddle until a little water sputters when dropped onto it. Cook the roti for about 2 minutes until browned and speckled on one side. Turn, spread with ghee or oil and cook, turning frequently, until baked – about 5 minutes in all. Lift the Roti out of the pan and clap it quickly between the palms to make it pliable. Wrap in a clean cloth to keep warm until the other Roti are cooked. Serve at once.

## ORANGE TEACAKE

Makes a 1 kg (2 lb) loaf

Preparation time: 15 minutes + 45 minutes cooking

*250 g (8 oz) plain flour*

*4 teaspoons baking powder*

*½ teaspoon salt*

*125 g (4 oz) sugar*

*1 tablespoon finely grated orange zest*

*2 eggs, beaten well*

*250 ml (8 fl oz) orange juice, strained*

*40 g (1½ oz) unsalted butter, melted and cooled, plus extra for greasing*

*This teacake, popular in Barbados and the English-speaking islands, is really orange teabread. It takes even less time to make than Banana Bread (page 78) and is light and delicious.*

Preheat the oven to Gas Mark 4/180°C/350°F. Butter a 23 × 12 cm (9- × 5-inch) or 1 kg (2 lb) loaf tin.

Sift the flour, baking powder and salt into a large bowl. Stir in the sugar and orange zest.

In another bowl whisk together the eggs, orange juice and butter. Fold this mixture gently into the dry ingredients with a spatula.

Pour the batter into the loaf tin. Bake in the oven for 45 minutes or until a skewer comes out clean.

Let the teacake cool in the tin for about 5 minutes before turning it out onto a wire rack to cool completely.

*Orange Teacake*
*Paw-paw Ice Cream*
*Avocado Ice Cream*

Serves 6–8

Preparation time: 20 minutes + 20 minutes or 6 hours freezing

### For the basic custard:

4 large eggs (size 1 or 2)

125 g (4 oz) sugar

250 ml (8 fl oz) single cream

250 ml (8 fl oz) milk

½ teaspoon vanilla essence

*Ice cream is popular everywhere and equally so in the islands, which rejoice in a great abundance of fruits to flavour the ice cream. Cooks on the island of Grenada worked out this simple formula for adding puréed fruit to a basic custard to make ice cream. If you are lucky enough to have an ice-cream freezer, this becomes a quick, simple and enticing dessert. It is even better served with the islands' Banana Bread (page 78) or Orange Teacake (page 84).*

In the top of a double boiler, off the heat, beat the eggs with the sugar.

In a small saucepan heat the cream and milk to scalding point. Stir the milk mixture into the eggs.

Add hot water to the bottom of the double boiler and cook over a very low heat, stirring constantly with a wooden spoon, until the custard is thick enough to coat the spoon. Leave to cool and then stir in the vanilla essence.

AVOCADO ICE CREAM Peel, stone and mash 2 ripe avocados, scraping all the flesh from the skins. Mix with 50 g (2 oz) of caster sugar. Add

1 tablespoon of lime or lemon juice and mix thoroughly. Stir into the basic custard and freeze for 20–25 minutes in an ice-cream freezer. Or freeze for up to 6 hours in a freezer, beating once.

BANANA ICE CREAM Peel and mash 500 g (1 lb) of very ripe bananas in a bowl until smooth. Stir in 1 tablespoon of lime or lemon juice. Fold into the basic custard and freeze as above.

GUAVA ICE CREAM Drain and purée canned guavas, sieve to remove any pips and then sweeten to taste if necessary. Stir 250 g (8 oz) into the basic custard. Freeze as above.

MANGO ICE CREAM Purée enough fresh or canned mango in a food processor to make 250 g (8 oz). Mix with 1 tablespoon of lime or lemon juice and 50 g (2 oz) of caster sugar. Add to the basic custard and freeze as above.

PAW-PAW (PAPAYA) ICE CREAM Purée enough canned or fresh ripe paw-paw in a food processor to make 250 g (8 oz). Mix with 1 tablespoon of lime or lemon juice and 50 g (2 oz) of caster sugar. Add to the basic custard and freeze as above.

PINEAPPLE ICE CREAM Mix 250 g (8 oz) of drained canned crushed pineapple in natural juice with 250 g (8 oz) of caster sugar. Add to the basic custard and freeze as above.

# SWEET FRITTERS

Preparation time: 5 minutes + 1 hour standing + 15 minutes cooking

*For the batter:*

*125 g (4 oz) plain flour*

*1½ teaspoons baking powder*

*¼ teaspoon salt*

*1 tablespoon caster sugar*

*4 eggs*

*2 teaspoons melted butter*

*2 teaspoons corn or groundnut oil*

*2 teaspoons white rum*

*For the fritters:*

*125 g (4 oz) mashed or thinly sliced bananas, drained and chopped canned or fresh pineapple or chopped mango*

*½ teaspoon vanilla essence (optional)*

*groundnut or corn oil for deep-frying*

*caster sugar for sprinkling*

*Sweet fritters are as popular as savoury ones (page 19) island-wide. Favourite fillings are mango, pineapple and banana.*

Sift the flour, baking powder, salt and sugar into a bowl. Make a well in the centre and break in the eggs. Add the butter, oil and rum and beat until the batter is smooth. Leave to stand at room temperature for 1 hour.

Mix the batter with either the bananas, pineapple or mango, and the vanilla essence if using. Drop tablespoons of the mixture into oil heated to 190°C/375°F on a frying thermometer. Deep-fry for 6–8 minutes until golden brown all over. Drain on kitchen paper, sprinkle with caster sugar and serve.

*Note*: If liked, shallow-fry the fritters. Heat 5 cm (2 inches) of oil in a frying pan until a teaspoon of the batter sizzles on contact and then fry the fritters until golden brown on both sides.

# DRINKS

## RUM PUNCH

(Pictured on page 5)        Serves 1

Preparation time: 5 minutes

2 tablespoons lime juice

4 tablespoons Simple Syrup (page 94)

6 tablespoons rum

125 ml (4 fl oz) water

3 or 4 ice cubes

a dash of angostura bitters (optional)

a pinch of grated nutmeg (optional)

a sprig of fresh mint, to garnish

*Rum is the king of drinks in the Caribbean, whether it is dark, white or golden. There are innumerable recipes, even for classics like Rum Punch and Planter's Punch (page 92). The formula for this punch from Barbados is very old, and very reliable whatever rum is chosen.*

Combine the lime juice, Simple Syrup, rum, water and ice cubes. Stir for a couple of minutes, strain and pour into a tumbler.

If liked, add a dash of angostura bitters and a grating of fresh nutmeg. Garnish with a sprig of mint.

## HOLIDAY EGGNOG

Serves 6–12

Preparation time: 10–15 minutes

6 eggs, beaten lightly

400 g (13 oz) can of sweetened condensed milk

finely grated zest of 1 lime or lemon

450 ml (¾ pint) white rum, preferably Trinidadian

1 teaspoon vanilla essence

a dash of angostura bitters

crushed ice, to serve

*Eggnogs using evaporated or condensed milk are island-wide, popular everywhere. An added bonus in the hot climate of the Caribbean is that they keep if bottled and refrigerated, useful when the demands of holiday entertaining are hard to gauge. This eggnog from Trinidad is too delicious to last very long.*

Combine all the ingredients, except the crushed ice, in a large bowl and mix thoroughly, whisking well. Pour into bottles and refrigerate until ready to use.

Serve the eggnog over crushed ice in punch cups. Use more ice for those preferring a milder drink.

# PETIT PUNCH

| Little punch | Serves 1 |
|---|---|

Preparation time: 5 minutes

1 tablespoon Simple Syrup
(page 94)

3 tablespoons white rum

a small piece of lime peel

1 or 2 ice cubes

*With its companion drink, Punch Vieux (Old punch), this is the most popular aperitif in the French islands. Its formal name is Punch au Petit Citron Vert (Punch with little green lime) or Punch Blanc (White punch). It is simplicity itself and is made with the local* rhum agricole, *a very gentle spirit,* jus de canne, *which is pure cane juice or syrup, and the zest of a small, very flavourful green lime. Punch Vieux is even simpler: just cane juice and rum with a little water and ice. Simple Syrup is the best substitute for cane syrup.*

Combine the Simple Syrup and rum in a small glass. Twist the piece of lime peel over the glass to release the oil and then drop it into the glass. Add one or two ice cubes and a little water. Stir gently to mix.

# PEANUT PUNCH

| | Serves 4 |
|---|---|

Preparation time: 5 minutes + 10 minutes cooking + 2 hours chilling

450 ml (¾ pint) milk

5 tablespoons smooth
peanut butter

sugar to taste

1 tablespoon cornflour

125 ml (4 fl oz) water

125 ml (4 fl oz) white
rum, or to taste (optional)

ice cubes, to serve

*Traditionally this peanut punch from Trinidad is a soft drink; however, many Trinidadians find it improved with the addition of rum.*

Combine the milk, peanut butter and sugar to taste in a saucepan. Cook, stirring with a wooden spoon, over a low heat to mix.

Mix the cornflour and water in a small bowl and stir into the peanut butter mixture. Continue to cook over a low heat for 3–4 minutes longer until thickened lightly. Leave to cool.

Pour the punch into a jug and refrigerate for 2 hours. If liked, stir in the rum before serving. Serve in small tumblers with ice cubes.

# BLUE MOUNTAIN COCKTAIL

Preparation time: 5 minutes

6 tablespoons white rum, preferably Jamaican

3 tablespoons vodka

3 tablespoons Tia Maria

4 tablespoons orange juice

2 tablespoons lime juice

6 or more ice cubes

*Blue Mountain coffee is famous for its flavour; so is Jamaica's coffee liqueur, Tia Maria, which gives this Jamaican cocktail a smoothly subtle taste.*

Combine all the ingredients in a cocktail shaker and shake vigorously. Pour, unstrained, into two glasses. Add extra ice cubes if liked.

# QUEBRAHACHA

Preparation time: 5 minutes

4 tablespoons white rum

2 tablespoons Curaçao or orange liqueur

1 teaspoon lime juice

2 dashes of angostura bitters

3 or 4 ice cubes

*This drink from Curaçao is named after a native Venezuelan evergreen tree that has emigrated to the island. Also called the Divi-Divi tree, all the branches lean to one side. Perhaps the implication is that the drinker will not remain entirely upright if too much Quebrahacha is drunk. The Curaçao used in the drink is made from the Seville (bitter) oranges that grow on the island.*

Combine all the ingredients, except the ice cubes, and stir well. Put the ice cubes into a glass and pour the drink over them.

# PLANTER'S PUNCH

Serves 1

Preparation time: 5 minutes

4 tablespoons Dominican rum, or dark rum from Martinique or Guadeloupe, or any dark rum

1 tablespoon lime juice

1 tablespoon Simple Syrup (page 94)

2–3 dashes of angostura bitters

4 ice cubes

1 maraschino cherry, to garnish (optional)

*The tiny mountainous island of Dominica, lying between Martinique and Guadeloupe, produces glorious dark rum and glorious limes. Here they combine to make a splendid punch.*

Combine all the ingredients, except the ice cubes, in a cocktail shaker and shake vigorously. Strain over the ice cubes into a small tumbler. Garnish with the maraschino cherry, if liked.

# PIÑA COLADA

Serves 2

Preparation time: 5 minutes

250 ml (8 fl oz) pineapple juice

125 ml (4 fl oz) fresh or canned coconut milk (page 10)

125 ml (4 fl oz) white rum

3 or 4 ice cubes

**To garnish:**

pineapple spears

maraschino cherries

*This Puerto Rican drink has become increasingly popular, though it is often mispronounced: piña is pronounced 'peenya' in Spanish. No matter, it is great for summer drinking.*

Combine the pineapple juice, coconut milk and rum in a cocktail shaker and shake vigorously several times. Strain into two highball glasses containing ice cubes. Garnish with the pineapple spears and cherries.

*Planter's Punch*
*Piña Colada*
*Frozen Daiquiri*

# DAIQUIRI

Serves 2

Preparation time: 5 minutes

175 ml (6 fl oz) white rum

2 tablespoons lime juice

1 tablespoon Simple Syrup (below)

3 or 4 ice cubes

*The Daiquiri is believed to have been invented in Cuba by American engineers after the Spanish–American war, though there may well be other stories about its origin. It began as a long drink but soon became cocktail-size. It has now been overtaken in popularity by the frozen Daiquiri.*

Combine all the ingredients in a cocktail shaker and shake vigorously several times. Strain into two chilled cocktail glasses.

*Variation*: For a frozen Daiquiri, use 250 ml (8 fl oz) crushed ice instead of the ice cubes. Combine the crushed ice with the other ingredients in a food processor or blender and process until the mixture has the consistency of snow. Serve immediately in two large saucer champagne glasses, with short straws.

# SIMPLE SYRUP

Makes about 450 ml (¾ pint)

Preparation time: 5–10 minutes

500 g (1 lb) sugar

450 ml (¾ pint) cold water

*It is worth making this simple syrup to use in drinks instead of sugar. It gives a smooth drink, is easy to make, and keeps. One tablespoon of the syrup is equivalent to 1½ teaspoons of sugar.*

Combine the sugar and water in a bowl and stir to mix. Stir from time to time until the sugar has dissolved.

Pour the syrup into a glass jar and keep in a cool place.

# INDEX TO RECIPES

Cover design: Barry Lowenhoff
Cover illustration: Sally Swabey
Text design: Ken Vail
Photography: Laurie Evans
Styling: Lesley Richardson
Food preparation for photography: Pete Smith
Map: Perrot Cartographics
Typesetting: Ace Filmsetting Ltd, Frome, Somerset
Printed and bound by Printer Trento, Italy